COSMIC!

NORTHERN ENGLAND

Edited by Michelle Warrington

First published in Great Britain in 1998 by
POETRY NOW YOUNG WRITERS
1-2 Wainman Road, Woodston,
Peterborough, PE2 7BU
Telephone (01733) 230748

All Rights Reserved

Copyright Contributors 1998

HB ISBN 0 75430 215 6
SB ISBN 0 75430 216 4

FOREWORD

With over 63,000 entries for this year's Cosmic competition, it has proved to be our most demanding editing year to date.

We were, however, helped immensely by the fantastic standard of entries we received, and, on behalf of the Young Writers team, thank you.

The Cosmic series is a tremendous reflection on the writing abilities of 8-11 year old children, and the teachers who have encouraged them must take a great deal of credit.

We hope that you enjoy reading *Cosmic Nothern England* and that you are impressed with the variety of poems and style with which they are written, giving an insight into the minds of young children and what they think about the world today.

CONTENTS

Belle Vue Junior School
Jennifer Glencross	1
Benjamin Blain	1
Stuart Glencross	2
Angela Minervini	3
Mark Sykes	4
Kate Dixon	5
Emily Neil	6
Lee Routledge	6
Robert Easton	7
Charlotte Park	7
Ben Simpson	8
Lisa Postlethwaite	8
Kristofer Lorimer	9
Nicola Irving	9
Sophie Russell	10
May Irving	11
Victoria Hill	11
Matthew Pattinson	12
Jonathan Paton	12
Kate Hughes	12
Vicky McDermott	13
Sarah Millican	13
Hannah Coates	14
Lauren Johnston	14
Michael Routledge	15
Alice Kean	15
Gary Stainton	16
Laura Woods & Jenni Awang	16
Beverley Atkinson	17
Stephanie Woodbridge & Sarah Little	18

Bellingham County Middle School
Cara Higgins	18

Bransty Primary School
    Jodie Basso   19

Dane Ghyll CP School
    Kirsty Creegan   19
    Christopher Wilson   20
    Jennifer Shaw   20
    Lee Murphy   20
    Jessica Jordan   21
    Bryony Hambly   21
    Alexa Cree   22
    Megan Dance   22
    Ian Dunstan   23
    Victoria Hughes   23
    Ben Atkinson   24
    Michael Steele   24
    Bayanne Olabi   25
    Ashleigh Kent   25

Dearham Primary School
    Jenny Daymond   25
    Hayley Cameron   26
    Carys Anne McKenna   26
    Marcus Blackburn   27
    Sarah Buckley   27
    Andrew Stamper   28
    Stephanie Blair   28
    Byron O'Donnell   29
    Samantha Thomason   29
    Nick James   30
    Phillip Deacon   30
    Kerry Blair   31
    Andrew Charlton   31
    Pamela Foster   32
    Stefan Miller   32
    Lee Devereux   33
    Stephanie Agnew   33
    Luke Kirkwood   33

Clare Rogerson	34
Matthew MacDonald	34
Melissa Smithson	35
Lynsey Martin	35
Christopher McClements	36
David Riley	36
Kerryl Carter	37
Julia Donald	37
Michelle Glasson	38
Andrew Irving	38
Michael Lister	39
Sonia Neale	39
Andrew Deacon	39
Scott Wigham	40

Druridge Bay County Middle School

Patrick Gray	40
Stephen Dimelow	41
Laura Quicke	41
Emma Anderson	42
Barry McMurdo	42
Sarah Douglas	43
Hannah Hay	43
Ruth Shaw	44
Peter Guy	45

Goodly Dale School

Stephen Moore	45
Oliver Wood	46
Hannah Mattinson	46
Sarah Seed	47
Holly Dawson	47
Callum Scott	48
George Holgate	48
Holly Dawson	49
Owen Scott	49
Thomas Ainsworth	50
Charles Milne	50

Bobak Skelly 51
Robin Dawson 51
Adam Green 52

Gosforth CE Primary School
Kerri Dudding 52

Grange CE Primary School
Matthew Burrows 53
Lauren Hale 53
Emma Jeffs 54
Gregory Brown 54
Rhiannon James 55
Daniel Laisby 56
Holly Rushton 56
Alison Robson 57
Marie McDermott 57
Richard Lawrence 58
Thomas Sewell 58
Paris Whittaker 59
Amy Worth 60
Louise Bowe 60
Rotha Satterthwaite 61
Michael Lawrence 62
Pennyanna Sarha Newell Foster 63

Grasmere CE Aided Primary School
Freddy Warne 63
Curtis Woodburn 64
Richard Fielding 64
Thomas Langley 65
Katie Fielding 65
Hannah Clark 66
Eleanor Nelson 66
Lee James Wood 67
Lucia Nelson 67
Zoë Tremeer 68
Sophie Warne 68

Ireby CE School
- Jane Gill — 69
- Kerry Mumberson — 69
- Robert J Watt — 69
- Sam Smeaton — 70
- Anna L Rudd — 70
- Andrea Iceton — 71
- Jeannie Fletcher — 71
- Anita Graham — 72
- Conor McKenzie — 72
- Emma Benson — 73

Kirkby Thore Primary School
- Phoebe Cassels — 73
- Adam Warwick — 74
- Peter Devine — 74
- Heather Hills — 75

Langwathby CE Primary School
- Katherine Bardsley — 76
- Sammy-Jo Cleminson — 76
- Emily Woodfield — 77
- Melissa Noble — 77
- Hazel Price — 78
- Matthew Swift — 78
- Meredith Whitton — 79
- Melanie Wilson — 80
- Johnny Lisle — 80
- Emma Wilson — 81
- Annie Hall — 81
- Holly Cleasby — 82
- Claire Thwaites — 83
- Rowan Frame — 84
- Vikki Bird — 84
- Sarah Lowthian — 85

Leven Valley CE Primary School
- Tammy Lawler — 85
- Sally Ann Devine — 86
- Becky Shaw — 86
- Joy Nicholls — 87
- Nicole McKeown — 88
- Warren Brookfield — 88
- Mandy Rose Christopher — 89
- Melissa Gray — 89

Old Hutton CE School
- Simon Brown — 90
- Gillian Petley-Jones — 90
- Christopher Saxon — 91
- Hazel Parsons — 91
- Jessica Stephenson — 92
- Adele Thompson — 92
- Victoria Robertshaw — 93
- Laura Escolme — 93
- Josie Blakey — 94
- Ross Payne — 94
- Daniel Finch — 95

Our Lady Of The Rosary RC Primary School
- Alexandra Kneale — 95
- David Woodburn — 96
- Lauren Langhorn — 96
- Laura Duffin — 97
- Alyssa Greenway — 98
- Emma Chalker — 98

Plumbland School
- Greig Hill — 99
- Colin Sessford — 99
- Helen Rutherford — 100
- Philip Shackleton — 100
- Tom Grant — 101
- Jon Ridley — 101

Calum Hill	102
Matthew Prior	102
Angela Irving	103
Jack Grant	103

Raughton Head CE Primary School
Philippa Colville	104
Rebecca John	105

Robert Ferguson Primary School
Dale Hedley	105
Carl Wills	106
Kevin Mulraine	106
Leanne Hardon	107
Nicky Falder	107
Jack Guyan	108
Hannah Stephenson	109
Rachel Bulman	109
Michael Handford	110
Stacey Brown	110
Cristie Lynnette Millican	111
Scott Davidson	111
John Blenkharn	112

St Begh's Junior School, Whitehaven
Luke Haslett	113
Kimberley Elliott	113
Lauren Shimmin	114
Jordan Wells	114
Jessica Thompson	115
Stephanie Parkinson	115

St Cuthbert's RC School, Windermere
Stephanie Woodward	116
Ross Santamera	116
Justin Pape	117
Sam Cleghorn	117

St Margaret's CE Primary School, Durham City
- Kate Buxton — 118
- Emily Ashfield — 118
- Rachael Stewart — 119
- Joy Rathbone — 119
- Leila Panesar — 120
- Shanaka Kahakachchi — 121
- Rebecca J C Lancelot — 121
- Jonathan Gordon Best — 122
- Louisa Kate Dobson — 122
- Katie Yeats — 123
- Lizzie Thomson — 123
- Sophie Dobson — 123
- Priya Prasad — 124
- Charlotte Hutchinson — 124
- Elizabeth Southgate — 125
- Julia Robson — 125
- Ami Sawran-Smith — 126
- Joanne Weeding — 126
- Will Evans — 127

St Monica's Preparatory School, Carlisle
- Aysha Rafique — 127
- Yasemin Padidar-Nazar — 128
- Sarah Colquhoun — 129
- Aoife Kieran — 130
- Pippa Stobart — 131
- Sarah MacDowall — 131
- Sarah Frost — 132
- Carolyn Koussa — 132
- Robert Swindells — 133
- Ben Smith — 134
- Richard Blacklock — 134
- Stephen Harris — 135
- Georgina Cregan — 135
- Claire Sevar — 136
- Victoria Milbourn — 136

Emma Sims	137
Jacqueline Haslam	137
Sophie Robson	138
Rachael Fletcher	138
Jack Stamper	139
Jamie Benzie	139
Geoffrey Smith	140
Katherine Lynch	140
Louise Irving	141
Jodie Parkhouse	142
Shardia Sahib	142

Trinity CE Junior School

Ellen Mattinson	143
Matthew Carter	143
Hetty Partington	144
Adrian J Read	144
Jonathan E Branthwaite	145
Deborah Paris	145
Robert MacKereth	146
Katie Green	146
Peter Scott	147
Rachel Fox	147

Vickerstown School

Hannah Moore	148

Wensleydale Middle School

Alison Knight	148
Amy Hutchinson	148
Nicola Cherkassky	149
Lance Allen & David Jagger	149
Christopher Campbell	150
Craig Martin	150
Laura Watson	151
Jennifer Tait	151
Rachel Aspinall	152
Caroline Elsey	152

Ross Wallis	153
Stephen Pape	153
Nicholas Turner	153
Alison Leese	154
James Banks	154
Becky Fawcus	155
Cara-Jade Johnson	155

Yarlside School

Matthew Higgins	156
Rachael Crewdson	157
Jennifer Southall	157
Katy Walker	158
Liam Roberts	158
Benjamin Shaw	159

THE POEMS

THE CUPBOARD UNDER THE STAIRS

I don't like the cupboard under the stairs,
It has creepy crawly spiders and grizzly bears.

I run very fast, when I go past
The cupboard under the stairs,
In case one of those grizzly bears
Breaks through the roof and grabs me by the tooth.

I don't like the cupboard under the stairs,
It has creepy crawly spiders and grizzly bears.

Jennifer Glencross (9)
Belle Vue Junior School

SKIING IN THE MOUNTAINS

The snow is soft
The sky is blue
The perfect place for me and you.
Put on your skis and whoosh, you're off
Down the mountainside, oh gosh!
That was steep,
And in a flash
You're upside down
Oh what a bash.
But up you get, it's such good fun
To ski in the snow up to your bum.

Benjamin Blain (9)
Belle Vue Junior School

SKIING ADVENTURE

Swish swish
He started to go down the steepest slope on the mountain
He got faster and faster
As he went down the track
As he went down the track his skis went out of control
He was getting very scared
He went into the forest next to a stream
He just missed a snowdrift that he did not see
He went over a lake of solid ice
He hit a branch and got covered with snow that tasted nice
Through the trees so white and bright
The end of the forest was coming near
You could see the light coming through the trees
After that he got a very big shock
Because round the corner he saw a very big rock
It was right in the middle of the track
He thought he was going to die
Till he saw a little path
The path was very small and steep
Then he got a little peep
Of the track stopping at nothingness
It didn't take him very long to notice that he was in the air
Then he started gliding across the sky
Next he hit the ground with such a bang the sky started to shake
Next he found himself in a chair
Being patted on the back by the skiing super star Sir Stuart the Bear
It didn't take him very long to realise that he was the best
Better than all the rest.

Stuart Glencross (11)
Belle Vue Junior School

COLOURS

Yellow is like . . .
The sun sizzling in the sky
Yellow sand lying on the beach
Leaves drifting down from trees

Red is like . . .
My gym club leotard
Mars in the night-time sky

Blue is like . . .
The waves roaring in the sea
The sky on a clear day
The blue of our school jumper

Green is like . . .
Dipsy on the Teletubbies
10 green bottles sitting on a wall
Grass whirling in the wind

Orange is like . . .
2 tangerines that are in my lunch box
The English book that I write in
Mercury beside the Sun

Purple is like . . .
A bruise on my leg
A nail varnish waiting to be bought
Tinky Winky in the Teletubbies.

Angela Minervini (9)
Belle Vue Junior School

GUY'S SONG

There's a fizz and a whizz and a dance in the sky,
There's some smoke and some spitting
in the air.
And the fireworks explode
Bang! Bang! Bang!

Remember, remember the 5th of November,
After this month it is December.

A waterfall comes down from the sky,
They're shooting, they're whirling, and twirling,
Guy's been thrown on the fire.

Remember, remember the 5th of November,
After this month it is December.

There's a fountain coming down from the sky,
There's a *pop! Boom! Fizz!*
and a sizzle and a fizzle.
They whistle, glitter and *zoooom!*

Remember, remember the 5th of November,
After this month it is December.

They're shooting there, and everywhere,
Red, green, yellow and purple.
Catherine wheels above the fire,
And luminous colours in the sky
falling to the ground.

Remember, remember the 5th of November,
After this month it is December.

They crackle, bash and snap to the ground
and finally they are dead.

Remember, remember the 5ᵗʰ of November,
After this month it is December.

Mark Sykes (10)
Belle Vue Junior School

WINTER WOOD

In a frozen winter wood,
An old oak tree stood,
Covered over with ice and snow,
The old frozen owl had nowhere to go.
The oak tree stood icy and cold,
As the snowflakes fell big and bold,
A little boy came to play,
With his sledge this winter's day.
The owl saw the boy approaching with his sledge,
The owl called out sitting on the hedge,
The boy heard the owl and went over to see,
The owl leant over and pecked the boy's knee.
The boy picked it up and took it home,
The owl was naughty and pecked the garden gnome,
But when the summer returned once more,
The owl once again swept the little wood's floor.

Kate Dixon (10)
Belle Vue Junior School

WHAT IS YELLOW?

Yellow is the colour of the sun in the sky
giving light here as time goes by.
Yellow is the colour of the chicks being born
mother hen is proud because of her little crowd.
Yellow is the rainbow in the sky
making clouds all colourful as they go by.
Yellow is the colour of honey
Winnie the Pooh eats it a lot.
Yellow is the colour of pollen in a flower
we sometimes see it as we give flowers a shower.
Yellow is the colour of autumn leaves scattered across the ground
as the wind blows near.
Yellow is the colour of melons in a stall
getting bought all the time in one day and night.

Emily Neil (7)
Belle Vue Junior School

NIGHT THINGS

Outside the night hangs silently over everything.
The whole place is full of thick black darkness.
Cats stealing along the garden wall,
Bats catching their midnight feast,
Ghosts looking for easy targets,
Figures prowling in the dead of night.

Lee Routledge (11)
Belle Vue Junior School

A Ghost House

Skeleton bones rattling,
Cobwebs in the corner,
Creepy crawlies dashing and darting,
In and out the holes in the broken floor,
Ghostly sounds echoing in the basement,
Makes your hair stand on end with fear,
Wooden wardrobe creaks open,
Skeleton bones fall everywhere,
White glowing figures coming at you,
Fading and disappearing away.

Robert Easton (8)
Belle Vue Junior School

Bedtime Companion

Curly bear curly bear
we will climb the stairs
Curly bear curly bear
it's time for prayers
Curly bear curly bear
let's climb into bed
Curly bear curly bear
you sleepy head
Curly bear curly bear
it's time to dream of fun and friends.

Charlotte Park (8)
Belle Vue Junior School

Colour Poem

Red reminds me of . . .
Blood oozing down my leg,
The fire burning on a cold winter's day,
The sign of 'no entry' beside the road.

Orange reminds me of . . .
The bright sun in the sky,
The brightly coloured orange cards,
An orange crisp packet lying on the floor.

Green is like . . .
An enormous caterpillar crawling along a wall,
Green peppers straight from the supermarket,
A piece of green paper turn when people rushed to get it.

Ben Simpson (9)
Belle Vue Junior School

My Tap

My little tap has got a cough,
Because it got turned on then off.
Water going round and then it comes out,
I'm sure it's ill without a doubt.
It gives a splutter and then a cough,
Then I have to knock it off.
I try again but still it splutters,
'Oh not again!' my mother mutters.

Lisa Postlethwaite (10)
Belle Vue Junior School

WINTER

Winter is cold,
with snow on the ground.
No leaves on the trees,
and a chill in the breeze.
Everything white,
so clean and bright.
Children all happy,
to play in the snow.
Hands all frozen,
but their faces aglow.

Kristofer Lorimer (10)
Belle Vue Junior School

POLAR BEAR

Polar bear, polar bear, clean and white,
drinks all day, and snores all night.
He hunts for fish, his favourite dish,
he plays with his friends on the ice.
They like to relax in the sun when it is nice,
Running around in the nice fresh snow.
He can't run very fast, he is very slow.

Nicola Irving (11)
Belle Vue Junior School

A Colour Poem

Red reminds me of . . .
    Sitting in front of a warm blazing fire on a cold frosty morn
    Eating strawberries in a hot summer sun
    Raspberry jam with white bread in a sandwich.

Green is like . . .
    The leaves on a tree in mid spring
    Grass on a field where rabbits hide in their burrows
    A carrot top just chopped off.

Blue is like . . .
    The coldness on top of Mount Everest in winter
    The sky on a sunny day
    A blue marker people use to vandalise with.

Orange is like . . .
    My orange coat my mum bought me from Newcastle
    A carrot waiting to be eaten
    An orange felt tip pen I colour with.

Yellow reminds me of . . .
    La La from the Teletubbies
    A yellow pen waiting on my desk alone
    A sizzling sun on a warm day.

Purple is like . . .
    A big bruise on my knee from when I fell over
    Tinky Winky from the Teletubbies
    Coloured paper waiting to be used.

Sophie Russell (10)
Belle Vue Junior School

COLOUR POEM

Yellow is like . . .

The sun shining brightly in the sky
A banana, the skin slowly being peeled off
A leaf gliding slowly to the ground in autumn.

Blue reminds me of . . .

Coming to school on a cold frosty morning
The sea, gliding softly on a calm day
Carlisle United's home strip.

May Irving (9)
Belle Vue Junior School

MY WATER POEM

Water is a splashy thing,
Dark and cool in a pool,
Lovely and wet when the sun has set,
In a tap nice and flat,
Cold and hot in a pot,
In a swampy salty sea,
In a dewdrop gold and green,
All the year from spring to spring,
Water is the nicest thing.

Victoria Hill (8)
Belle Vue Junior School

UNDERNEATH MY BED AT NIGHT

Underneath my bed at night
There's lots of things that give me a fright.
Creepy crawly shiny things,
Bony fish with skeleton fins.
Half a dried pear, an old smelly sock,
Waiting for me to give it a wash.

Matthew Pattinson (10)
Belle Vue Junior School

STARS

The glittering light,
In the dark dark night,
Form a beautiful pattern,
Which is quite a sight!

Jonathan Paton (10)
Belle Vue Junior School

A SUMMER HOLIDAY DREAM

Take a stretch of sun and sand
Add a slice of sunshine.
Add a stinging jellyfish,
Sprinkle with the silver sea.
Cover with a coat of sand,
And wrap in moon and stars
To look at on summer nights.

Kate Hughes (8)
Belle Vue Junior School

MY WATER POEM

Water is a splashy thing,
Dark and cool in a pool,
Lovely and wet when the sun has set,
In a river brown and clear,
In a cloud fluffy white,
In a tear so clear,
In a raindrop lovely and cool,
In a wave very splashy,
All the year from spring to spring
Water is the splashiest thing.

Vicky McDermott (9)
Belle Vue Junior School

QUIET

Trees rustling, reflective water,
Slippy rocks, moss on the trees,
Crystal clear, the water shimmers,
The rapids up above, crashing down,
Splosh, the waves suddenly turn into dripping drops,
I feel happy and good inside me,
I feel I could fly because I feel so light,
It is so quiet, I could go to sleep
With the birds singing in my face,
I hear cars far away, then it stops,
I am all alone.

Sarah Millican (9)
Belle Vue Junior School

THE SEASONS

Spring
The time of year when new life begins
People are amazed at God's wondrous things.

Summer
Everyone out enjoying the sunshine
Smiling faces having a fun time.

Autumn
Everything around us begins to wither
People dreading that cold wintry shiver.

Winter
Snowy, ice and frosty things
People longing for the new begin of spring.

Hannah Coates (10)
Belle Vue Junior School

THE SEA GIRL

The sea girl lives by the sea,
As silent, as silent as can be,
She never talks,
She never sings,
She's all alone,
Now she's gone,
Why?
No one knows.

Lauren Johnston (10)
Belle Vue Junior School

JACK FROST

Jack Frost is a very icy man
He freezes things from side to side
And freezes us as well.
Colours silver and white
Sparkle lovely at night.
We just look out of the window
And see Jack Frost in the light.
He leaps from side to side
Freezing all the lovely shapes
That makes the garden glowy.
Jack Frost is a very icy man
He freezes things from side to side
And freezes us as well.

Michael Routledge (7)
Belle Vue Junior School

QUIET SOLITUDE

As I sit and watch the birds go by,
I see them singing in the sky.
As the sun shines on the stream,
I think it's almost like a dream.
The rough bark of the trees,
Swinging in the gentle breeze.
It makes me feel I have to be quiet,
And not make an awful riot.

Alice Kean (8)
Belle Vue Junior School

WRAPPING GRANNY

Rappin' granny,
She's a sure good thing!

I wrapped her up
and I threw her in the bin!

The bin man came,
She went to Spain,

and I've never seen poor old granny again!

Gary Stainton (9)
Belle Vue Junior School

WITCH'S SPELL

Leg of man, skull of rat
Witch in a ditch with a black and white cat
Blood of lizard, cat in slime
The witch has made a terrible crime.
Mixed together in a black and white pot
Sprinkled with bones that are boiling hot
Used by me in the dark by a light
Used to ruin people's sight.

Laura Woods & Jenni Awang (10)
Belle Vue Junior School

THE ALPHABET POEM

A is for Andrew who picks his nose
B is for Bev who likes to pose
C is for Craig who has smelly feet
D is for Diane who likes to eat
E is for Eddie who is very fat
F is for Fiona who sat on her cat
G is for Gavin who can't tell the time
H is for Hazel who hates to smile
I is for Ian who cannot swim
J is for Judith who goes to gym
K is for Kevin who plays football
L is for Linda who is very tall
M is for Mark who is so cute
N is for Nicola who plays the flute
O is for Oliver who likes Mickey Mouse
P is for Peter who lives in a house
Q is for Quentin who doesn't brush his teeth
R is for Rachel whose dad is called Keith
S is for Steven who has no hair
T is for Tracey who sleeps with a teddy bear
U is for Una who has a pet snake
V is for Victor who fell in the lake
W is for Wilma who is always in bed
X is for Xena whose favourite colour is red
Y is for Yvonne who likes to sing
Z is for Zac who wants to be a king.

Beverley Atkinson (10)
Belle Vue Junior School

WITCH'S SPELL

Eye of cat, leg of bat,
Skull of owl, tongue of rat,
Stir it, mix it, in a big black pot,
Bubble, bubble, till it's steaming hot,
Sprinkle, stir, with a star of night,
Put in a potion of bad eyesight,
Used on a baby at 12.00 hour,
Death is to come on my own good power.

Stephanie Woodbridge & Sarah Little (10)
Belle Vue Junior School

THE STRANGE MAN WHO LIVED IN OUR CARAVAN

The strange man
who lived in our caravan
had a strange old car
that wouldn't go very far!
He works with computers
and does this and that
but he doesn't have animals
not even a cat.
When he came for Christmas dinner
he wore a kilt which looked a winner.
After Christmas he moved
in such a good mood
and we saw no more of
the strange man
who lived in our caravan.

Cara Higgins (10)
Bellingham County Middle School

SPIDER

It's quiet, the room is empty,
I sit in the corner of the room,
I weave my web so big,
But someone's coming!
Yes someone's coming!
I crouch in the corner.
I don't know what to do,
A little boy comes and plays with a tool,
He's hurt himself now,
I crawl down beside him but he screams with fright,
His mother comes with a newspaper,
She swats me!
I'm dead!

Jodie Basso (8)
Bransty Primary School

MY WASHING MACHINE

My washing machine is like a baby,
very hungry.
The water is like the sea,
splashing around.
It sounds like a car
left running.
The clothes are like food
moving around in our tummies.
Then it stops so still and quiet
like night-time.

Kirsty Creegan (10)
Dane Ghyll CP School

THE ARROW

The arrow is a bullet flying in the air.
The arrow is a deadly weapon.
The arrow is a pointer showing the way home.
The arrow is the speed of lightning coming from my bow.
The arrow is like a branch from a tree.

Christopher Wilson (10)
Dane Ghyll CP School

A VACUUM CLEANER

A vacuum cleaner is like an
Aardvark eating ants,
Sucking the corners.
A vacuum cleaner is like a
Monster roaring,
Under chairs and round the curtains.

Jennifer Shaw (10)
Dane Ghyll CP School

UNTITLED

There once was a boy called Rod
Who had a big green toy frog
He put it in the pond
Which was very wrong
Because it sank to the bottom like a log.

Lee Murphy (9)
Dane Ghyll CP School

The Moon

The moon is like a diamond
on a black cloth.
It shines up the town
like a shiny sparkling eye.
It is like a street light
shining so bright in the sky.
It is like a big lump of cheese
shaped like a circle.
It's a football light
and shines down on people.
Big shadows fall across the street
like monsters from the moon.
The moon is like a juicy lemon
in a black bowl.

Jessica Jordan (10)
Dane Ghyll CP School

The Stars

The stars are tiny pieces of glitter,
kicked into the sky.
The stars are a shattered mirror,
reflecting the sun.
The stars are God's precious jewels
hung high in the sky.
The stars are fairy dust,
sprinkled from a magic wand.
The stars are Heaven's lampposts,
lighting up the night.
The stars are gold coins
lighting up the world!

Bryony Hambly (10)
Dane Ghyll CP School

THE WIND

The wind arrived like a piece of ice or snow on a cold winter's day.
It was as though a cape had been draped onto the town.
Like the whole sky was alive, as alive as you or me.
As the wind passed through and left the town as it rolled away,
The people stare and shout hooray.
Then like before the town was peaceful once more.
I caught up with the wind as it rolled onto another town far away.
There has never been a wind like that again
And I am still waiting for the wind to come back one day.

Alexa Cree (10)
Dane Ghyll CP School

FAIRIES AND BUTTERFLIES

Fairies are delicate as are their wings,
Just like butterflies, beautiful things.
They are very different, but can be the same,
None like flying out in the rain.

They're both sweet and colourful,
And shouldn't be touched,
Soft and wonderful, loved very much.
Fairies are quick and move without sound,
Unlike butterflies, they're never to be found.

Megan Dance (10)
Dane Ghyll CP School

ME AND MY DAD

Me and my dad are like two peas in a pod most people say.
I just came from nowhere one day.
We get on brilliant he said.
I am as good as gold.
He looks after me when I've got a cold.
When Dad picks me up
He says I'm light as a feather.
He puts me on the chair
And we watch television together.
It's time for bed.
My feet feel like lead.
'Up you go' Dad says, 'no messing about
Close your eyes and go out like a light.'

Ian Dunstan (10)
Dane Ghyll CP School

THE NIGHT SKY

Last night I went out to see the night sky.
I saw a silver coin,
This was the moon.
It lay on a piece of black velvet.
The stars which surrounded this big silver coin,
Are millions of diamonds
Twinkling on the velvet cloth.
So if you look into the night sky,
All you will see is the material of a black sparkly dress.

Victoria Hughes (10)
Dane Ghyll CP School

THE SUN

The sun is like an orange dinghy
Kicked high in the sky.
It is like a gold milk bottle lid
Floating in a pie.
It is like a gold boat
Going swiftly on its way
In the calm calm bay.
It is like a glistening bauble
Hung lonely on a tree.
It is like a piece of tinsel
Floating on the calm sea.

Ben Atkinson (9)
Dane Ghyll CP School

DIFFERENT ALIENS

Aliens come from far and
beyond the galaxy.
The are fat and thin,
small and tall.
Black and white,
stupid and clever.
Aliens are like people
from Earth,
They are all different.

Michael Steele (9)
Dane Ghyll CP School

THE TIGER

A tiger is a thunderstorm catching its prey,
It is a zebra staring at me,
It is a cheetah in a race,
It is a racing car at 100 mph.

Bayanne Olabi (9)
Dane Ghyll CP School

ICE-CREAM

There once was a girl of Barrow,
Who said 'We'll have ice-cream at Harrow.'
She said to Priscilla,
'I'll have a scoop of vanilla,'
Then said 'We'll go back to Barrow.'

Ashleigh Kent (10)
Dane Ghyll CP School

LOUD AND NOISY

Loud and noisy
is my dad snoring.
Loud and noisy
is the rain pouring.
Loud and noisy
is my sister who's boring!

Jenny Daymond (8)
Dearham Primary School

My Mum

A coffee-maker
A Co-op worker
A good driver
A good baker
A good gardener
A tear-drier
A warm-hugger
A care-taker
A good talker
A dish-washer.

Hayley Cameron (8)
Dearham Primary School

Morning Sounds

Alarm clock ringing.
Birds are singing.
Mum and Dad talking.
Baby brother screaming.
Postman whistling.
Cornflakes crackling.
Spoons clinking.
Fire smoking.

Carys Anne McKenna (8)
Dearham Primary School

MY DAD

A hard worker
A good reader
A good father
A rugby player
A motorbiker
A woodworker
A book reader
A good character
A paper reader
A tickle-maker.

Marcus Blackburn (8)
Dearham Primary School

LOUD AND NOISY

Loud and noisy
Is the mower cutting the lawn.
Loud and noisy
Is the wall being torn.
Loud and noisy
Is the farmer's horn being blown.
Loud and noisy
Is the cockerel calling at dawn.

Sarah Buckley (8)
Dearham Primary School

MY DAD

A good footballer
A farm worker
A giggle-maker
A tickle-tormenter
A lazy sleeper
An excellent fixer
A bike rider
A big scoffer
A car driver
A trip-taker.

Andrew Stamper (8)
Dearham Primary School

MORNING SOUNDS

My dad crunching a biscuit.
Alarm ringing.
The switch clicking on the wall.
My sister switching on the TV.
Music blaring.
Phone ringing.
Knocking at the door.
Splashing taps.
The kettle that clicks.

Stephanie Blair (8)
Dearham Primary School

MY DOGS

Spike is a very boisterous
Pal of mine he is.
I like to take him for walks.
Kind of timid, yes he is.
Excited, yes! Never calm.

A naughty little pair of pups.
Never behave, not at all.
Don't like being alone.

Toby is a little pup.
Obvious I think it is.
Boring he is, you must be joking!
Young - yer; about four and a half months.

Byron O'Donnell (9)
Dearham Primary School

RED AND WHITE

Red and white
are tropical fish.
Red and white
is the pattern round my dish.
Red and white
is the dress I wear.
Red and white
is the bobble in my hair.

Samantha Thomason (8)
Dearham Primary School

My Mam

A TV-watcher
A Coventry supporter
A good ironer
A good footballer
A bossy boots
A good sewer
A good washer-upper
A car driver
A warm hugger
A good dancer.

Nick James (8)
Dearham Primary School

Morning Sounds

Alarm clock bleeping,
My brother's ladders creaking,
Bang of the door,
Thudding downstairs,
Click of the toaster,
The bacon crackling,
Mum and brother shouting,
My dog barking.

Phillip Deacon (8)
Dearham Primary School

I'm a Terrifying Ghost

I'm a terrifying ghost
I'll scare you for certain
I'm in between a monster
And an old net curtain.

I imitate a bat, then horrify a cat
I can float around the room
And jump over the moon
As long as I frighten you.

I can frighten you by growing and shrinking
And turning bright purple
I can scare you at night
Are you frightened? No.

But what do you expect
I'm only half a metre high.

Kerry Blair (10)
Dearham Primary School

Morning Sounds

Alarm clock ringing.
Birds tweeting in the trees.
Dad and Mam chattering.
Car's engine brumming.
Dad slurping his coffee.
Mam crunching cornflakes.
My dog growling.
Dishwasher rattling.

Andrew Charlton (8)
Dearham Primary School

ANIMALS IN DANGER

Animals are in danger,
North, and south animals too,
Indian elephants,
Monkeys,
Apes living in the zoo,
Lions and tigers from Africa,
Snakes which squeeze so tight.

Never will they live,
Even if we fight,
Elephants are in danger,
Dinosaurs are extinct.

Horses need to live,
Elephants need to give,
Leopards might just make it,
Please help the animals!

Pamela Foster (10)
Dearham Primary School

SOFT AND QUIET

Soft and quiet
is when my sister sleeps.
Soft and quiet
is when my sister eats.
Soft and quiet
is the letterbox rattling.
Soft and quiet
is the radiator gurgling.

Stefan Miller (8)
Dearham Primary School

My Dog Midge

Midge is brave and mighty too.
He can run a mile in just a while.
He never ever bites
Because he has a fear of heights.
He is so small, he will never grow tall,
Just like his best friend too.
He will dare to jump off London Bridge.
That's why we call him Midge.

Lee Devereux (9)
Dearham Primary School

Ice-Cream

Melting ice-cream in the town
All the dogs are looking around.
When all the dogs come
They get their snouts out and about.
Up and down they look,
But still they have no luck!

Stephanie Agnew (10)
Dearham Primary School

Snow

Snow covers the treetops,
All over the ground, it is all around.
Snow is soft like cotton wool.
It makes a crunch when you step on it.
Making patterns in the snow
Is so much fun to play around.

Luke Kirkwood (10)
Dearham Primary School

MY DREAM

I have a friend called Zag,
He lives on Planet Zog.
He's got a dog called Zug,
It sleeps on my rug.
I've known him for a day,
We have fun when we play.
He's coming round today at four,
We'll have fun some more.
He's got three eyes, four legs,
He juggles with seven eggs.
It was just a dream,
I'll finish my ice-cream.

Clare Rogerson (10)
Dearham Primary School

SPRING!

The beginning of spring -
But a few weeks ago
All the hilltops were covered with snow.
Trees and bushes were so bare
Not a single flower there.
Now I can see the lambs skipping
And hear the birds singing.
Now there's a new life in everything.
How I love the beginning of spring.

Matthew MacDonald (10)
Dearham Primary School

What The Seasons Mean To Me

School mornings
Lambs making noises
Children listen to workmen sawing
And children making funny noises

School is out
Children shout
And play merrily all about
The evening goes on and it all dies out

Bonfire night and Hallowe'en
Witches come to scare children clean
On one autumn day every year
There is always Hallowe'en
And children are always fresh and clean

Christmas time is in this season
Frost is on the leaves and children jump
And listen to them crunch
Children finish their last lesson
To pick snowdrops in a bunch.

Melissa Smithson (11)
Dearham Primary School

Rabbits

Fluffy furry things
Cuddly, friendly pets like toys
Eat carrots and hay.

Lynsey Martin (10)
Dearham Primary School

FIVE TINY MICE

Five tiny mice sitting on the floor,
One thought he smelled a cat,
Then there were four.
Four tiny mice hiding in a tree,
One lost his footing,
Then there were three.
Three tiny mice playing in the bathroom,
One fell in the loo,
Then there were two.
Two tiny mice riding on a swan,
One slipped and fell in,
Then there was one.
One tiny mouse sitting all alone,
Suddenly he saw the cat,
Then he was gone.

Christopher McClements (11)
Dearham Primary School

WINTER

W inter's cold, winter's wet, sun is what we never get
I cy roads and icy lakes, knocking knees and the shakes.
N ights are longer, shorter days, look across the hills and you'll see a haze.
T iny bits of frosty flakes, a nice cup of tea and nice hot steaks.
E very time I go outside, I go on a sledge to have a ride.
R obins sitting on the fence in the morning, while I'm still in bed snoring.

David Riley (11)
Dearham Primary School

I LIKE ANIMALS

I like animals, I think they're cute,
Dogs, cats, rhinos, hippos in the zoo,
I love them like they are my own pets,
Except for rats and snakes,
I could not do without animals,
'Cos some of them are my mates.
Pets keep you occupied,
Also fit and healthy,
If some people didn't have dogs
They would not be so wealthy.
Dogs are very helpful to the deaf and blind,
They bark for the phone,
They sometimes get a bone,
For being so good to people.
Some animals are becoming endangered,
Although they look so beautiful in the wild.
The flight of a bat,
The miaow of a cat,
I would miss so much.

Kerryl Carter (10)
Dearham Primary School

SWEETS

Sweets melt in your mouth
They can make your mouth water
And children love them.

Julia Donald (11)
Dearham Primary School

SEASONS

What winter means to me:
Cold dark nights
Frost glittering on the trees
Snow soft and white on the ground
That's what winter means to me.

What spring means to me:
Daffodils sprouting in the grass
Lambs springing in the field
Green leaves growing on the trees
That's what spring means to me.

What summer means to me:
People lazing in the sun
Children having water fights
Long, hot, shining days
That's what summer means to me.

What autumn means to me:
Crunchy brown leaves on the ground
Wrapped up warm on cold days
Whistling winds blow away your hats
That's what autumn means to me.

Michelle Glasson (10)
Dearham Primary School

KILLER WHALE

Renowned for killing
Misunderstood animal
Caught by the poachers.

Andrew Irving (11)
Dearham Primary School

Dolphin

Swims through the ocean
Just like a speeding bullet
Sleek and grey dolphin.

Michael Lister (10)
Dearham Primary School

Tiger

T he striped colours on its back
I gnoring visitors
G iant creature athletic and powerful
E legantly walks down the bank
R ound and round its territory.

Sonia Neale (11)
Dearham Primary School

Ants

Crawling on the ground
Dragging food along the earth
Busy colony.

Andrew Deacon (10)
Dearham Primary School

RHINO

R hinos are in danger of becoming extinct.
H umans poach them every day.
I n the plains of Africa
N o rhino is safe
O n this planet!

Scott Wigham (10)
Dearham Primary School

ALONE

How different life would be for me,
Without my friends and family.
No one to get me out of bed,
No one to punch me in the head.
(My sister's favourite occupation)
No clocks, no tellies, no time for bed,
Unfamiliar routine instead.
Always eating,
Friends at the door,
Will these things happen no more?
My treasured pets to be neglected,
Cold and wet and looking dejected.
No more football,
No more goals,
Instead I'm just a lonely soul.
Nothing to take me from 'A' to 'B'
No car, no train, nor lorry.
No pencil or paper to keep me amused,
Instead I will be bored and confused.

Patrick Gray (11)
Druridge Bay County Middle School

THINGS I WOULD MISS

The warm welcome of my dog,
The warm laughter of my friends,
The feel of my cat's tickly fur on my face,
The friendly voice of a friend on the telephone,
My favourite songs played loud on my stereo while I
                          read my best loved book.
The instant fun of games on computers and watching
                          telly in front of a warm log fire.
A turkey roast drenched in hot gravy,
Cricket played by the castle,
Football in winter - muddy and fast.
These are the things that I would miss.

Stephen Dimelow (12)
Druridge Bay County Middle School

A HALLOWE'EN NIGHT

There was once a wicked witch,
Who had a big, big twitch,
She scratched and she scratched until it was red,
But still she couldn't go to bed
And the next day it was black 'n blue,
So she scratched it again and her friends helped her too.
One day she recovered from that twitch.
Now she is a proper witch.

Laura Quicke (9)
Druridge Bay County Middle School

THINGS I WOULD MISS

Watching leaves float to the ground,
And the noise rain makes, like a tapping sound.
Beautiful flowers gently swaying in the wind,
The feel of fur next to my skin.
The smell of chestnuts being roasted on the fire,
And the strong desire to touch smooth glass.
The crackling noise of wood as it burns,
The flames of a fire as they tumble and turn.
The reflection of the sun on a still lake,
And the smell of cakes when they've just been baked.
The sight of a sunset slowly fading away,
When you eat cream on a hot summer's day.
The nipping of the winter frost,
Which changes the landscape and makes me lost.

Emma Anderson (12)
Druridge Bay County Middle School

BONFIRE NIGHT

On the fifth of November,
We light up the sky,
With bangers and rockets which zoom up high.
Catherine wheels go round and round,
Their colours reflecting on the ground.
We have fun on bonfire night,
Watching the flames burning bight,
The flames will soon consume the guy,
Because every year he must die.

Barry McMurdo (10)
Druridge Bay County Middle School

HAVE YOU SEEN MY WOODLICE?

Have you seen my woodlice in the playground?

Have you seen my woodlice anywhere around?

Have you seen my woodlice creeping up your wall?

Have you seen my woodlice making a great big fall?

Have you seen my woodlice crawling along the floor?

Have you seen my woodlice knocking at your door?

Have you seen my woodlice creeping up your chest?

Have you seen my woodlice chewing up your vest?

Sarah Douglas (10)
Druridge Bay County Middle School

THINGS I WOULD MISS

Cool bright wintry days on the mountain tops,
Ronan and the other bands live on Top of the Pops,
Those sunny, warm evenings eating ice-creams,
Watching Manchester United beat those teams,
My music loud every night,
My mother shouting at my brother, 'Get out of sight!'
All these things I love and would miss,
And future things like Ronan's kiss!

Hannah Hay (11)
Druridge Bay County Middle School

MISSING THEM

I would miss touching:
The warm, silky feel of my cat's fur,
The cushioned softness of my mum's hug,
The smooth velvety coat of my bedtime teddy,
And the gentle, loving end of day kiss.

I would miss seeing:
A brightly coloured rainbow in a hazy blue sky,
The kind, friendly faces of my family,
The ever changing programmes on television,
And the magnificent green scenery of the Scottish Highlands.

I would miss smelling:
The fuzzy, peach soap of my morning wash,
The fresh, crusty rolls straight from the oven,
A dewy pile of freshly cut grass,
And the sweet, lasting perfume of fuchsia in a vase.

I would miss tasting:
The red, thick, tomatoness of sauce
On the crispy skin of long, thin chips,
The juicy, crunchy bite of a Cox's Pippin,
And the rich, brown, luscious flavour of chocolate.

I would miss hearing:
The sound of birdsong in the morning air,
The happy laughter of my best friends,
The dancing music in a loud disco,
And voices talking, talking, talking together.

Ruth Shaw (11)
Druridge Bay County Middle School

THESE I HAVE LOVED

Imagine how it would be,
No one to talk to, nothing to see,
The things I would miss would surely be,
The touch of friends and family,
Next it would have to be,
The taste of my mother's tea,
Also I would have to say,
I'd miss football every day,
All my friends think of each other,
I'd miss going fishing with my brother.

Peter Guy (11)
Druridge Bay County Middle School

BONFIRE NIGHT

Flames flickering furiously into the air.
Spitting sparks, shuttling all around.
Bonfires crackling and burning in the night.
Flames swaying in the cold, gentle breeze.
People eating toffee apples with sticky mouths.
Red and yellow flames creating black smoke
Which pollutes the air.
Children and grown-ups watching the guy being
Gobbled up by hungry flames.
Hot smoke and cold air making everything go
Fuzzy in front of your eyes.

Stephen Moore (9)
Goodly Dale School

PERILOUS POLLUTION

Seas overflowing with oil oozing out on top of the sea.
Spilling uncontrollably from the tanker.
The sea life disappearing to other islands, only the bravest come back.
All the plants around it die and wither.
The ducks are covered in oil, saturated in it.
Killing wildlife.
The waves become still,
Because of the heavy oil taking the life from the water,
Weighing it down.
The birds cry out pitifully for help.

Oliver Wood (8)
Goodly Dale School

THE SUNSET

Smoothly blending into different colours.
Gleaming in your face, and a twinkle in your eyes.
The bright light spying on you and silently, mysteriously dies.
Like a butterfly gliding down to earth.
Watch the glimmering path of light, sink slowly . . . slowly out of sight.
See birds flying into their nests, ready for a good night's rest.

Hannah Mattinson (8)
Goodly Dale School

THE SPACE ATMOSPHERE

Unknown planets spiralling through space.
Aliens plodding away from the flames of rockets as they pass.
Glittering stars acting like street lights to guide the way
                                for the shining satellites.
Sitting in planets of different shapes and sizes are gouged out footsteps.
Aliens have hundreds of languages that spacemen don't understand.
The sun is feared because of the heat it gives to space.
At night I feel as though the stars are my good friends.
Tree branches swaying, trying to catch stars,
                    reaching up to the heavens.
Strange lights flash in a dark night sky.

Sarah Seed (9)
Goodly Dale School

THE LONG RIVER

The river flows slowly.
It floods and shifts stones to the side.
It breaks things in half.
The river shines in the sun.
It glistens too.
The ducks swim happily in it.
When you look, you can see your reflection.
It takes people's lives away.
Rivers give us water to drink and wash.
We can swim in the crystal clear water on a summer's day.

Holly Dawson (8)
Goodly Dale School

Muddling Machines

Saws whacking the wood,
Twisting, turning wheels carving closely.
Power searching engines, breaking the heavy metal.
Shuddering, shaking spikes.
Jagged edges sticking out.
Vibrating motors leak out noise.
Smashing and pummelling golden metal until it's thin.
Wrecking, the revving motors are bashing, and breaking
                                                up the ground.
Hijacking the cars' burning lights,
Then smashing them into smithereens.
Whirling and twirling, up and down.
Spinning the fiddly gadgets everywhere.

Callum Scott (8)
Goodly Dale School

Machinery

Spinning wheels whirling and swirling.
Power surging engines clanking and clinking.
Sparks flying as the saw shudders from side to side.
Pistons blowing, valves banging and then hissing.
Starting up suddenly,
Then *bang, bang,* breaking down with a deafening thud.
The smell of burning rubber smouldering,
As the belts break without warning.

George Holgate (9)
Goodly Dale School

FOGGY DAYS

Fog sneaks around the place, looking for somewhere to hide.
It sneaks out from behind objects.
It frightens people.
It slithers through tiny holes that no one else can squeeze through.
Fog comes from clouds.
It seems white just like mist.
Fog likes to cover places to make them disappear.
People crash their cars too.
It hides the stones and posts in fields.

Holly Dawson (8)
Goodly Dale School

JELLYFISH

Jellyfish are mysterious, luminous creatures,
Floating around under the murky depths of the sea.
Silently creeping through the water,
Beautiful but deadly,
Moves so slow and sleekly,
Slipping back through the darkness,
Going, going, gone.

Owen Scott (10)
Goodly Dale School

RIVERS

Rivers start calm going down mountains,
Getting rough, crash, bang, crash down waterfalls,
Fish swimming through currents,
Jumping over waterfalls,
Rapids battering stones,
Tributaries joining the mighty river,
The river's come to an end heading towards a lake,
The river hits the lake and that's a river's journey.

Thomas Ainsworth (10)
Goodly Dale School

RIVER'S FLOW

A river flows with speed.
A river takes lives.
A river holds animals, such as salmon.
The salmon leaps.
It gets polluted.
Rivers give us lovely sorts of waterfalls that sparkle.
Rivers reflect the sun.
Rivers slither through rocks and cracks.
They flow often with a fast current.
Rivers are deep and gloomy.

Charles Milne (8)
Goodly Dale School

RIVERS RUSH

Rivers bend, rivers rush.
Water creating rapids.
Dark creatures are living underneath.
It sprays up.
It's as if it wants to be in charge.
Clear as crystals, down so deep.
It flows along.
It side-steps, then it stops.
The stones stop like a traffic jam.
When the mountain rainfall comes, the
                river becomes a torrent.

Bobak Skelly (9)
Goodly Dale School

RIVERS

Rivers can be very sleek.
But sometimes rough.
Rivers create waterfalls.
Rivers sometimes overflow.
Most rivers come from springs up on top of mountains.
A river is like a roller-coaster.
The water in the river is nice, cold water.
In the winter the river ices up.
In the summer the river glistens.

Robin Dawson (9)
Goodly Dale School

RIVERS

Rivers flowing fast.
Rivers splashing.
They stretch so wide.
The surface is frosty, full of bubbles.
They fall quickly like little waterfalls.
They wind narrowly sometimes.
When the weather is bad, they get rough.
When the weather is good, the water shines.
The water can be deep, reflecting the river bed.

Adam Green (8)
Goodly Dale School

THE CHINA MOUSE

The china mouse
Sits at home
All alone.

In his little box,
Out of the window
He sees a fox.

Somebody who's in a dash
Knocks the table
And smash.

Now our little mousy friend
Finally comes
To a sad end.

Kerri Dudding (8)
Gosforth CE Primary School

NEW FOOTBALL BOOTS

I have got some new football boots,
I am always scoring goals.
They are expensive,
I am always kicking balls.

They are magic boots,
They have got red flaps on the front.
On the tip of my boots they are not sharp,
They are blunt.

My new football boots are very clean,
Only sometimes though.
Last week our team lost,
Oh no!

Matthew Burrows (9)
Grange CE Primary School

AS I LOOK OUT THE WINDOW

I see something strange,
A cat and a mouse playing some games.
They're playing checks, they're playing chess.
Goodness knows what they will do next.
Oh no, it's happened.
It can't be true.
Now the cat has gone bazoo.
Now he's realised that his checkmate could make him fat.
So back to normal (reality).
The cat chased the mouse up a tree.

Lauren Hale (9)
Grange CE Primary School

POLLUTION!

Once I asked my dad,
'Is pollution bad?'
He answered, 'Yes,
That was a good guess!'
Then I started wondering,
At school I was pondering,
How could we stop this pollution?
Then I heard of the Greenhouse Effect,
And how the world, they were trying to protect.
So now I'm on the other side,
And I'm full of pride,
I try to stop
Our world going pop,
With pollution from us,
And every car, lorry and bus
From now on I'm going to respect,
The Greenhouse Effect!

Emma Jeffs (10)
Grange CE Primary School

MOTORCYCLIST

I am a motorcyclist,
I ride and ride,
I am so fast,
That I zoom across the tide.

I am a motorcyclist,
I crash and crash,
I am so nervous,
I get bashed and bashed.

I am a motorcyclist,
I get people cross,
I am so dangerous,
I have not got a boss.

I am a motorcyclist,
I am a diver,
I am a doctor,
I am going to be a car driver!

Gregory Brown (9)
Grange CE Primary School

I WANNA BE SMART

I wanna be smart
I wanna be neat
I wanna be brill
I wanna treat
I wanna travel round the world
I wanna have my hair curled
I wanna be cool
I wanna have my own private pool
I *don't* wanna go to school
I wanna go to the moon
And ride in a hot air balloon
I wanna be really ace
And blast off into space
I wanna be on TV
I wanna be a VIP
I wanna be smart
I wanna be *Me!*

Rhiannon James (9)
Grange CE Primary School

THE MAN FROM BOMBAY

A man from Bombay walked over Morecambe Bay
When the children saw him
They crowded round him
And said, 'Hey, you're from Bombay.'
'Hey, I know I am from Bombay.'
And while he was talking,
He heard the children squawking,
Hey, there are some people walking.
'Hello,' he said.
'I am from Bombay.'
And he said, 'Hey, I am sinking.'
So the people could not stop blinking.
And the man from Bombay walked back over Morecambe Bay,
And said, 'I will never come here again.'

Daniel Laisby (9)
Grange CE Primary School

CHOCOLATE

I love chocolate, chocolate is yummy
Chocolate tastes great in my tummy.
Chocolate is cool, chocolate is ace
If you eat chocolate you'll win every race.
Chocolate is brown, chocolate is sticky
But chocolate is really very licky.
Chocolate drink, chocolate ice-creams
I think of chocolate even in my dreams.

Holly Rushton (10)
Grange CE Primary School

ZOMBIES

Lime green, purple, orange and blue, these are the colours of zombies,
Lime green eyes staring at me,
Purple antennae wobbling around on top of their blue heads,
An orange body wobbling around on top of a blue pair of legs with blue arms stuck on the side,
They're slowly walking towards me,
What will happen to me now,
Will it be pain or will it be gain,
I slowly walk backwards towards the spaceship,
I climb in hurriedly and watch the zombies slowly disappear into thin air,
I fly back home to earth eating pizza all the way,
Slice by slice, I could eat it all day.

Alison Robson (10)
Grange CE Primary School

I WANNA BE A POP STAR

I wanna be a pop star,
I wanna sing lots of songs,
I wanna be famous,
I wanna meet lots of famous people,
I wanna sing my best songs.
On second thoughts I wanna be *me*.
I wanna drive a massive car,
I wanna be a millionaire,
I wanna have fish and chips,
I wanna buy fashion clothes.
On second thoughts I wanna be *me*.

Marie McDermott (9)
Grange CE Primary School

LITTLE STUPENDO

Little Stupendo has a bike,
He has it because he does not want to hike.
There is a motor right at the back,
Also there is room for a rucksack.

Little Stupendo makes a track,
He makes the track out at the back.
Also he goes to school on it,
He does not like cars one bit.

On his bike there is a light,
He is a little short on his height.
Stupendo smiles on his ride,
He nods his head from side to side.

His big brother has a bike,
His small brother has a trike.
Big bro has a shiny outfit,
Little bro has no kit.

But Stupendo is dead now,
His replacement is a cow.
The cow does not have a bike,
But he knows how to hike.

Richard Lawrence (9)
Grange CE Primary School

IF I HAD A HAMSTER

If I had a hamster,
I would call him Jack,
I'd even buy him a rucksack,
I'd buy him a clown,
And a dancing bear,
I think I would buy him a singing hare.

He would live in a lane,
And right next door would be a big fun fair.
He would have a place to swim,
And a big full size gym with all the things inside.
He would be quite tall with a bouncing ball,
And all the sport things you can buy,
You see I don't want him to be sad.

Thomas Sewell (10)
Grange CE Primary School

DO SOMETHING

At last, someone to confide in,
I am sick of stupid humans polluting me.
Spraying harmful greenhouse gases,
Blowing exhaust fumes about.
Dropping litter and chopping trees down.
Don't they realise how harmful it is?
How bad it is for them?
How I hate it?
How I will become too delicate to live on?
I heard the other day that the parks will be
Wiped out by 2999 if we don't do something soon.
There is so much smog in big cities people are dying.
I've tried telling it to adults, but they either don't care or they
                                        don't believe me.
They are slowly, bit by bit, wiping out fish, birds, mammals,
                    rainforests, deserts and much, much more.
But now I've told you, a child, the future of us all.
Please do something, I know you can.
So do something, please, please, *pleasssse!*
Do something or you will die and so will I!

Paris Whittaker (9)
Grange CE Primary School

INJECTION FEARS

Fears are things you don't overcome,
Everybody has one, except for some,
One of mine I hate to admit,
I really don't like it one little bit.
Everybody hates them, they're a real pain,
But you have to have them again and again.
I wish they wouldn't be around,
That would suit me down to the ground.
I'm in the waiting room,
Then the doctor booms,
'Next please!'
Oh no, not me, I'm not having that,
It's worse than being bitten by a vampire bat,
Ow! There, it's been in and out.
It's not that bad, so please don't pout!

Amy Worth (10)
Grange CE Primary School

I WANT TO BE A SPACEMAN

I want to be a spaceman,
And boom up into space,
I want to visit Pluto,
And go to another place.

I want to be a spaceman,
And float up in the sky,
I want to see the stars and moon,
And see the Earth go by.

I want to be a spaceman,
And fly to the sun,
And sizzle all my sausages,
And eat them in a bun.

I want to be a spaceman,
And fly home to Mum,
This has been really ace,
And I've had loads of fun.

Louise Bowe (10)
Grange CE Primary School

WHY?

These are the questions of my life,
Why does the world spin on an axis?
Why do we have to sleep?
Why do we die and where do we go?
Why don't we live forever?
Why does time pass so quick?
Why can't it just stand still?
Why do we have to go to school?
'To learn,' say the grown-ups. It's so boring.
Why aren't we just born clever?
Why are there spellings?
Why are there tables?
Why are there teachers who always say *work?*
I don't know why.
But one thing I know is that without these
Why! Life would be boring.

Rotha Satterthwaite (10)
Grange CE Primary School

ROCKET MAD!

They call me Sam
Man I'm cool;
I'm just a great big
Rocket flying fool!

I'm 12 years old,
I play with guitars;
My friend called Jim
Once came with me to Mars!

I've made a diary
Of what I've seen;
I've even made
A super space machine!

My dad's a pilot,
Mum's one too;
So what's a kid
Supposed to do?

My pal named Chris,
Said with a yawn,
'A flyer isn't taught . . .
He's born!'

Michael Lawrence (9)
Grange CE Primary School

KOALA BEAR
(Dedicated to Axel Cook Foster)

A koala is not a bear,
I've told you once, so there.
It eats eucalyptus leaves
Because it likes them.
It loves them, the leaves make sugar,
It is a clever bear.

A koala is not a bear,
I've told you twice so there.
It's nice and cuddly,
It's got a sweet face,
It climbs up trees
At its own slow pace.
But my koala is not real
It sits there near some orange peel.

A koala is not a bear,
It's a *marsupial!*

Pennyanna Sarha Newell Foster (10)
Grange CE Primary School

SPACE INVADERS

Sail to the stars, meet lots of aliens
They are here I scream.
With purple eyes, and big, big, ears.
They live on Jupiter in big purple holes.
We will get eaten alive!
They are yellow and they have blood all over them.
Keep away.

Freddy Warne (7)
Grasmere CE Aided Primary School

SPACE

Zooming through space what a brilliant place,
Seeing stars and don't forget Mars,
I'm going to the moon, very soon.
Earth's a place where you can surf in the air, I don't care
In space, that's my very cool place.
Here comes a comet, I'd better bomb it.
There's a light, it's very bright
It could be a meteorite, I must be right!
I'm having my lunch in which there are pies,
Oh look there's a monster with three big eyes.
It's very black, like I'm in a sack.
I'm looking around, there's not a sound.
Going to the sun, I bet it is fun,
But it might burn my bum!

Curtis Woodburn (11)
Grasmere CE Aided Primary School

COSMIC

5, 4, 3, 2, 1, *blast-off*
The spaceship takes off.
I am an astronaut
All I can see is an empty black space.
Suddenly, there were stars surrounding me.
Clusters of galaxies shine in an unorganised pattern.
Where could I be?
Maybe in a constellation?
Good, I'm safe on the planet Mars.
Help! There's aliens charging towards me
And they look ugly and I want to go home.

Richard Fielding (8)
Grasmere CE Aided Primary School

OUTSIDE OUR EARTH

Outside our earth of land and sea,
Where people reign like you or me.

Go out of there and you shall find,
Not just an empty space within your mind.

But where you can use it to extremes,
With nebulae and comet streams,
Where you can look upon your dreams.

When you are up in solar space,
You can look upon the face of the moon.

Planets like Jupiter, Venus and Mars,
Dodge between the shooting stars.

On the sun the gas loops ruled,
Its red-hot temper never cooled.

Back to our earth of land and sea,
Where people reign like you or me.

Go to there and you shall find,
An amazing planet, planet mild and kind.

Thomas Langley (10)
Grasmere CE Aided Primary School

SPACE

Space is a big black void.
There's so many planets it makes me annoyed
There's Jupiter, Venus and Mars
The constellations and then all the stars.
I like the moon as dusk takes the light.
It shines so bright in the middle of the night.

Katie Fielding (9)
Grasmere CE Aided Primary School

COSMIC

Up in space,
It is a wonderful place,
With all the stars
Venus and Mars.
Planets floating all around me,
Neptune, Saturn and Mercury.
In my rocket I sit and look,
Lots of pictures I have took.
Of the planets up so high,
Higher I go through the sky.
But when you think the sun is a star,
Up in space so far.

Hannah Clark (9)
Grasmere CE Aided Primary School

COSMIC

Cosmic, cosmic, planets all around,
Cosmic, cosmic, holes in the ground.
Cosmic, cosmic, man on the moon.
Cosmic, cosmic, alien on the loose.
Cosmic, cosmic, we are really near Saturn.
Cosmic, cosmic, the ring is a lovely pattern.
Cosmic, cosmic, I'm running out of air,
Cosmic, cosmic, I'm flying in the air.

Ahhh! I'm falling
Phew, I'm safe
But where am I
Oh, I'm home and safe.

Eleanor Nelson (8)
Grasmere CE Aided Primary School

Cosmic

The shooting star is like a space shuttle zooming through space,
I want to be a rocket, roaring and ripping its way to Mars.
Powering on to Saturn, the seven rings reflecting off my shining metal skin.
One of the rings looked like a UFO but it was just my imagination, only illusion.
As I fall to Earth, I begin to burn my way through the atmosphere,
Extreme and intense heat surrounds me, only for a short while then the clouds cool me down.
Ready for the splash down, ready for the fall.
Now I'm sad because my journey is finished and I'll never fly again.

Lee James Wood (9)
Grasmere CE Aided Primary School

Do You Ever Look At The Stars

Sometimes if you look carefully,
You can see the Plough,
Sometimes you can see shooting stars
zooming through the air.
Saturn is amazing with its seven rings of gas
and is very chilly.
Mars and Venus are nearest to Earth.
Earth is the only planet with humans living on it.

Lucia Nelson (9)
Grasmere CE Aided Primary School

IS MARS...

Made out of chocolate bars
I'd have a super day
Eating my way through the Milky Way
I wonder if you have to pay an entrance fee
To choose your very own chunk of the Galaxy
Do you think the Moon's made of cheese
Would it taste nice dunked in Mum's herbal teas
If I eat this massive feast
It would make me a mega-beast.

Zoë Tremeer (10)
Grasmere CE Aided Primary School

UNIVERSE

U ranus is the one that people laugh at.
N eptune has a god named after it.
I f you're cold don't go to Pluto.
V enus is closest to the Sun.
E arth is where we live.
R ed is the colour of Mars.
S aturn has seven rings round it.
E very planet has a name like Mercury or Jupiter.
   We are only a tiny part of the Universe.

Sophie Warne (11)
Grasmere CE Aided Primary School

ANGRY

The colour is red as a rose,
The taste is like a hot and spicy turkey curry,
It smells like chilli,
It sounds like music on full blast.
It feels like I could hit someone.
It looks like a very mad bull.

Jane Gill (11)
Ireby CE School

SPRING

In spring the snowdrops grow with the yellow daffodils,
Lambs are born white as snow,
Horses graze on the green, green grass,
Pigs laze around in the mucky, mucky sty,
The chicks peck at the corn, corn, corn,
The cattle stand in the cattle shed,
Mooing, mooing, mooing, all day long.

Kerry Mumberson (11)
Ireby CE School

EMBARRASSED

When you're embarrassed your cheeks glow red,
That is the colour of your feeling,
It loves to give other people a laugh,
When it does it gets satisfied,
Then it stops for now,
After that it will have another go!

Robert J Watt (10)
Ireby CE School

I'M AN ANGRY MAN

I walked through the door,
Threw my bag on the floor.
Stomped up the stairs,
Tore the head off my teddy bear.
Turned my room upside down.
I went outside for some fresh air,
I felt like shooting a hare.
I took some deep breaths,
And went back inside.
'Sam! What have you done to your room!
Tidy it up right now!'
I'm an angry man again.

Sam Smeaton (11)
Ireby CE School

THE SQUIRREL

I once saw an endangered red squirrel,
His tail was as thick as a fiddle,
He had a coat of rusty red,
From the tip of his tail to his head.
His two little, black eyes,
Twinkled like stars in the night skies.

He scurried amongst the fallen autumn leaves,
And found plenty to eat with great ease,
He stored them away for another day
And then off he went to play.

Anna L Rudd (9)
Ireby CE School

School

Down in ye ancient school,
Children scream, 'This is doom!'
Waiting for that special word.
Playtime, playtime, run, skip, jump!
Teacher's whispering, 'Don't come back!'
I'll be glad to see their backs!
Teachers scratching the blackboard,
They're driving me up the wall.
Go home, go home, I can't take any more!
Don't come back, I'll only dislike you more.
'Cool!' they say, 'Lots of fun no more school,
It's boring, it's no fun.'

Andrea Iceton (11)
Ireby CE School

Summer To Winter

The birds are singing in the sky,
Early waking in July.
The sun is rising in the east,
Morning has dawned with absolute peace.
The seas are calm, the wind has no breath.
Gliding birds have great release
As the long, hot summer days decrease.
Toward the fall and winter's beast.
The dark will reign, the cold will freeze
We'll all dream of next summer's ease.

Jeannie Fletcher (8)
Ireby CE School

WINTER GLOW

As the world changes from season to season,
It's weird,
Suddenly it is hot then it's cold.
No one knows the reason,
When summer seems old.

When you put your bikes away,
Your sledges come out,
hoping for snow,
so that you can go
and play and shout!

Winter brings snow
Winter brings ice
But there isn't anything
quite as nice as watching the winter glow.

Anita Graham (10)
Ireby CE School

SAD

I wish I buried myself in the cold, cold ground,
Sometimes I wish I ran the speed of sound.

But it's fairly useless, my wishes won't come true,
Which makes me very angry, and very, very blue.

I wish I was friendly, helpful and a lover,
Instead I've got an ugly, psychopathic brother!

Conor McKenzie (10)
Ireby CE School

MY DOG

I have a dog, his name is Tag,
His coat is brown and furry,
I take him out most every day,
Such fun we have, we run and play,
Such clever tricks my dog can do,
I love my dog, he loves me too.

Emma Benson (10)
Ireby CE School

MY BLACK HORSE

I had a horse,
I had a black horse,
grazing in the meadow, eating grass.
I had a horse,
I had a black horse,
standing in the meadow feeding its foal with its fresh
rich milk.
I had a horse,
I had a black horse
that loves me.
I had a horse,
I had a black horse,
I love her.

Phoebe Cassels (7)
Kirkby Thore Primary School

DINOSAUR

There is a dinosaur coming and
there is panic in the street,
my mum said if we were good
we could see it for a treat.

There is a dinosaur in the street,
and it's about to eat.
It's eating all the cars,
it's eating all the buses.
Now he's walking down the street
to see what all the fuss is.

Adam Warwick (7)
Kirkby Thore Primary School

PIRATES

Pirates are scary, like a shark.
Pirates are strong as can be.
They sail through the dark.
They feel like they are going,
a thousand miles, knowing
that the sea is fast.
Will it last?

Peter Devine (9)
Kirkby Thore Primary School

THE GREEN NYMPH

A dry, old orange snake was giving a green nymph a lift to her home,
When suddenly out jumped a blue giant gnome.
'Help, help,' said the gnome, 'There is a wizard come and see.
He is going to blow up our tree.'
Oh, I'll come and take him away,
But only if you pay.
Anything just take him back to where he came from
I will magic up a big, black bomb.

So *abracadabra,* come bomb, come,
There appeared a big black bomb that was bigger than a giant's thumb.
Then came out the wizard pot,
Then with a mighty throw,
Crash, bang, blow.
The wizard flew, left and right,
The big explosion was so, so bright
I felt the hot, hot heat,
On my tiny feet.

Everyone cried out, hip, hip, hooray,
The nymph said now where's my pay.
You can be the queen for a week,
We will buy you a nice dress and you will be chic.
So hour after hour,
The nymph was treated like a flower,
After the week,
The nymph set up home on the mountain peak.

Heather Hills (10)
Kirkby Thore Primary School

HELP OUR WORLD

Now hear me! Can you look back and see our old world, can you?
With the green grass and the blue, and animals, birds and fish.
I can't, you need to slow down.
I can't see the hills and the blue sky from my window.
In fact, I bet you have forgotten what it used to be like.
From my window I can see cars with smoke,
Supermarkets with meat from the animals.
Most of the man-made things are making Earth worse.
Why can't we live as it was?
Or don't you like it as it was?
You greedy people, all you want is money.
I remember when birds used to nest on my roof and sing.
Now they are flying around trying to find somewhere to nest.
So please stop. Slow down and think.
   Help our world!

Katherine Bardsley (9)
Langwathby CE Primary School

STUNNING SATURN

Almost as big as Jupiter,
And Jupiter has belts of swirling gas,
Clouds cover its surface which is
Made of a mixture of liquids and fumes.
Bands of storm clouds surround Saturn
Giving it a ringed appearance.
It has a solid core surrounded by ice and hydrogen gas.
Saturn's rings consist of millions of fragments of ice,
Coated rock floating in space.
I think that Saturn is the most spectacular planet of all.

Sammy-Jo Cleminson (8)
Langwathby CE Primary School

AMAZING NEPTUNE

You're going to Neptune, you're leaving Earth behind.
It looks tiny. You're coming up to rusty red Mars.
Now we are leaving it and coming up to giant Jupiter
With its red spot, whizzing around and leaving Jupiter behind,
Coming to stunning Saturn spinning around with its many rings.
We are coming to Uranus. It is blue and green
Because it is made out of gas and water.
We are coming to Neptune. It looks blue
So it is named after the Roman god of oceans.
You think the surface is solid. You take a step.
You fall through. You cry 'Help!'
But nobody hears you.

Emily Woodfield (8)
Langwathby CE Primary School

AN ALIEN GUIDE TO BABBIES

Good morning class.
Today we are talking about babbies.
You feed babbies where they have tongues.
They listen from what you call hearing aids.
They smell from nosels.

They wear clothes and little tiny footwear.
Blue for boy babbies and pink for girl babbies.
They are bald with little hairs on their heads.

Babbies make this funny noise called wailing.
We are going to visit planet Earth to see a real babbie.
That is the end of my lesson today.

Melissa Noble (8)
Langwathby CE Primary School

WALKING ON THE MOON

Walking on the moon,
Jumping, bounding,
Flying . . . almost,
Swaying, swinging,
On the moon.
Footsteps from the astronaut before me,
My footsteps,
Dusty, dreary,
The moon.
Me only the twelfth person to walk on the moon.
I see the Earth shining above,
My home,
Always my home,
But the moon,
It's something different,
Not my home,
But my friend.

Hazel Price (9)
Langwathby CE Primary School

STOP POLLUTING OUR WORLD

Stop polluting our world, are you listening?
You are killing our ozone layer,
And you are letting the sun's harmful rays in.
You are killing God's animals and killing us!
You are killing trees and animals
Which live in the rainforests.
Please stop.

It may look beautiful out there
But you're polluting it.
By your factories and cars like
Your Volvos, your Peugeots and
Your buses and your wagons.
So stop polluting our world!

Matthew Swift (7)
Langwathby CE Primary School

OUR WORLD

Listen to me,
We are damaging our world.
Our amazing world.
Please look at our world,
Just think, in a few years' time nothing will be left.
Nothing!
Cars killing animals on the road,
Chopping down trees for bigger motorways.
Our greediness.
Factory men dumping chemicals in the sea.
Killing animals.
Stop, think, if your were a dolphin would you want to be killed?
Our selfishness.
Fresh air gone forever,
Do we want people with asthma to suffer?
People living on the streets,
Would God want this?
They cry for help but we ignore them.
Why?
Our world!
Do we really want this poverty?

Meredith Whitton (9)
Langwathby CE Primary School

The Comet

Shining, silvery comet
goes past the hot sun.
Past Mercury,
closest to the sun.
Past Venus.
Past the Earth,
our home planet.

Past Mars, the red planet.
Past jumbo Jupiter.
Past storming Saturn.
Past tipped Uranus.
Past blue Neptune.
Past faraway Pluto.

But no one knows where it is going
shining, silvery comet.
It might crash,
silver tail following it.

Melanie Wilson (8)
Langwathby CE Primary School

Comets

Comets shining brightly,
I wonder why they go shooting past.
Do they have fuel to make them go so fast?
When will the next one show?
Will I be alive to see it glow?

Johnny Lisle (8)
Langwathby CE Primary School

THE SPACESHIP FROM PLUTO

It came down from space
his head was all green,
his hands were all crinkly,
like something not seen.

They came out of their spaceship
in a straight single file.
There wasn't a sound
not one gave a smile.

Sarah said 'This is so much fun.'
Claire said 'We won't walk, let's run.'

The aliens said 'My brother's dead.'
And when we all got home we went back to bed.

Emma Wilson (9)
Langwathby CE Primary School

JUPITER

Jupiter is big, Mercury is small,
Jupiter is the biggest of them all.
You think Mercury is small?
Pluto is the smallest of them all.
You think Jupiter has the most rings,
Uranus has eleven, it has most of all.

Annie Hall (9)
Langwathby CE Primary School

THE SPACE RACE

Whooshing through space,
at a very fast pace,
it is very exciting,
the gravity is fighting

Stars shooting by,
and I say goodbye,
to the Earth,
as it flies out of sight.

Venus, Mars and Jupiter,
are all flying into view,
as well as twinkling constellations,
Orion, the Plough, the North Star too.

The race is nearly over,
my journey's almost done,
and all I have to do now,
is to guarantee I've won.

An extra burst of power,
to see me to the moon,
I'm getting a little tired now,
so I hope I get there soon.

Hooray! I've won the race,
because I went at a very fast pace,
so now I shall set off home,
the space trophy is my own.

I know a place,
it's called outer space,
there're comets, meteors and stars,
but the man in the moon,
I will visit again soon,
because he lights up the night sky so bright.

Holly Cleasby (9)
Langwathby CE Primary School

PLANETS

Mercury
A hot little planet.

Venus
A grey dull planet.

Earth
Our home planet.

Mars
The red planet.

Jupiter
The big planet.

Saturn
The beautiful ringed planet.

Uranus
The tilted ring planet.

Neptune
The blue planet.

Pluto
The faraway planet.

Claire Thwaites (9)
Langwathby CE Primary School

STARS

You think that stars are small
Well, lots of things are smaller.
Our sun is a star
And it's very hot.

Our Earth, compared to the sun
Just looks like a spot.
And the sun isn't the biggest star
One sun just looks like a dot.

Now you're thinking that stars are big
But some things are actually bigger.
To cross our Milky Way
Would take much more than a day.

But here's the biggest thing
That our galaxy is in . . .
The universe!

Rowan Frame (8)
Langwathby CE Primary School

IN THE MIDDLE OF THE NIGHT

Up in space in the middle of the night
the aliens got up and started to fight.

One boy was the only one there
except for the aliens that gave him a scare.

The boy ran and the aliens ran faster
caught the boy, he was called The Master.

The boy was brave, he gave a wave
and the aliens ran away.

Vikki Bird (8)
Langwathby CE Primary School

SATURN

S aturn oh Saturn you are so warm.
A re you a planet with two rings?
T urn off the heat before I faint.
U p in space so far from Earth
R un away far from home.
N ever go because
   I'll miss you!

Sarah Lowthian (8)
Langwathby CE Primary School

A THOUSAND YEARS ON

We dream about a whole new world,
Where lands of secrets have been unfurled.
With robots chasing us around,
Lots more planets have been found.

Holidays on the moon,
In every garage there'll be a Rock-oon.
Spacesuits for sale in every shop,
Factories everywhere go *whizz, bang, pop!*

You'll hear people argue,
What's a giraffe, an elephant, a kangaroo.
Look at the pollution,
What have we done?
Our world's not the same for anyone.

Tammy Lawler (11)
Leven Valley CE Primary School

MY LITTLE CHINA DOLL

I had a little china doll
Her hair was shiny gold
And when I looked into her eyes,
She winked at me like so.

I loved my little china doll
I took her everywhere
I even took her to the park
And the country fair.

I lost my little china doll
On a sunny day.
I don't know where she's gone
I think she's run away.

Sally Ann Devine (10)
Leven Valley CE Primary School

THE LITTLE WHITE RABBIT

I look across the sunny meadow
There is a little stream
But there
I see a very small figure
Drinking at the stream.
Its whiskers are twitching
It has sea-blue eyes
It is as white as snow
There are butterflies fluttering by.
It turned its head
And fled.

Becky Shaw (10)
Leven Valley CE Primary School

WHEN I WAS THREE

When I was three
I had a friend,
That asked lots of questions,
Like why bananas bend,
Or why the moon is round.
I couldn't answer all the questions,
Because I was only three.

When I was three,
I had a ball,
That I always played with,
But one day,
He ran away,
And he was lost forever.

When I was three,
I had a gigantic toy box,
That I kept everything in.
One day I looked through my
Toy box.

On my fourth birthday,
I had an enormous cake,
The cake was huge and glistening,
When I looked on top,
There was something I had seen before,
It was my little friend.
Then I answered all his questions,
Because I wasn't three,
I was four.

Joy Nicholls (9)
Leven Valley CE Primary School

IN SPACE

In space it's deep and dark
In space it's cold
What will I meet what will I see
On this exploration?

Up into space it's really scary.
Higher and higher as I look up,
All the planets glowing
Aliens fuzzing about.

It's time to return to the planet
I know
So I'm all safe, really safe,
Where all my friends are.

Space is really exciting
I've really enjoyed myself
I might just come back
To this wonderful, wonderful world.

Nicole McKeown (11)
Leven Valley CE Primary School

THE LITTLE SWIMMING MAN

There was a swimming man, who swam a great big length.
On the way he raced a whale, where he needed a load of strength.

When he won he shouted 'Hip Hip Hurrah!'
He won a cup, as big as a truck and he needed a crane to carry it away.
But the crane couldn't manage it, it coughed and spluttered,
And the next thing the cup had smashed.

Warren Brookfield (9)
Leven Valley CE Primary School

MANATEE

Whoosh went the boat gliding across the sea,
Whack, bang, swipe and whip the propellers hurting me.
I am 45 million years old I am a manatee,
Nobody thinks of us when they poison our sea.

Now I feel the pain much more,
I've stopped trying to swim.
I just drift down to the seabed
And soak under the sand.

Soon I close my eyes, I can taste the blood,
I really don't want to die this way,
I wish I had a say.

Mandy Rose Christopher (11)
Leven Valley CE Primary School

THE FROG

The joyful frog jumps up and down
He hops and leaps and plays around
He sleeps on a lily
And it's really quite chilly
But he's happy and has lots of friends

At this time of year
They disappear
To lay some new frogspawn
But in a few months
They will be tadpoles.

Melissa Gray (10)
Leven Valley CE Primary School

SPECIAL ME

Special me
I am unique
Not a commoner in the crowd
Standing out like a thunder cloud
Against a blue sky
A single light in the darkness
I am special me.

My own special abilities
No one else may have
My own style
My own methods
My own ways of life
I am special me.

No one looks, acts, walks like me
Talks or feels like me
The future is bright
I am special, I am me!

Simon Brown (10)
Old Hutton CE School

WINTER WONDERLAND

The sun sparkled on the snow,
A snowman stands silent
The frost stains the windows,
Sparkling, shimmering, silent snow
Snow like stardust flutters down,
Sharp green spikes push through the snow.

Gillian Petley-Jones
Old Hutton CE School

SPECIAL ME

I am special, special am I
I have feelings
Like no one else,
I play golf
Like no one else.

I work at school,
I play at home
like no one else,
I'm sad and happy
like no one else.

I like to listen,
to tapes and CDs
like no one else,
the future's bright
I am special, I am me.

Christopher Saxon (11)
Old Hutton CE School

MY GRAN SMOKES

My gran smokes,
I think it's all a big hoax,
I wish she would stop,
Because she's going to pop,
My brother does not like the smell,
But I can hardly tell,
I'm not joking,
But please stop smoking.

Hazel Parsons (10)
Old Hutton CE School

Snowdrops

Short green stork,
Soft white petals.
No pollen lies upon,
The soft white petals.
The screams of them as,
One by one gets plucked from the ground.
They stand tall and proud upon,
The fresh green grass.
Like soldiers ready for battle,
But soon the end has got to come.
I do not know but let's hope late,
For the snowdrop brings us great
Pleasure.

Jessica Stephenson (11)
Old Hutton CE School

Spring

Buds are sprouting everywhere,
Birds making nests with all their care.
A great burning yellow sun,
Children playing having fun.
Snowdrops with lots of drooping heads,
Daffodils in rows and beds.
Lovely chocolate Easter eggs,
Newborn lambs with black and white legs.

Adele Thompson (8)
Old Hutton CE School

TOYS

When you are tucked up in your bed at night,
your toys play but stay out of sight.

When you are tucked up in your bed at night,
if you hear a bump or a bang it's only the toys so
don't get a fright.

They dance and sing while the moon shines bright
and they may even sometimes have a fight!

When you are tucked up in your bed at night,
they have such fun making sure they tidy up before
daylight.

When you are tucked up in your bed at night.

Victoria Robertshaw (8)
Old Hutton CE School

SPECIAL ME

There is only one of me in the world,
I am special because I am me,
I am funny and ticklish,
I am medium sized,
The only me in the world
      That's me.

I laugh with my friends,
I laugh when someone tells me jokes
      That's me.

The future is bright
I am special, I am me!

Laura Escolme (9)
Old Hutton CE School

MY MUM

My mum is loyal and kind,
Gives us pocket money on Saturday night,
Takes us on holiday and trips every year,
She's good at maths and lots of other things too,
She's helpful, she buys us presents for birthdays,
Makes our favourite food (sometimes),
Sometimes embarrassing as well as special.

My mum is special, sometimes fussy,
When my room is in a tip my mum tidies it up for me (sometimes).
When we are in trouble Mum's always there.
She plays games sometimes,
She takes us on trips every week,
That's all about my mum.

Josie Blakey (10)
Old Hutton CE School

WINTER TIME

Green shoots like pea pods
Sticking through the ground.
Jack comes early in the morning
He leaves a bitter slidy water slope
Winter is a quiet lonely bitter place
Fires keep on burning through the day
Animals are asleep keeping warm
Your eyes go purple when you come in
from a walk
Footprints in the snow
Winter time turns into nothing
Then spring comes.

Ross Payne (10)
Old Hutton CE School

FURNESS ABBEY

Old, in ruins, Furness Abbey,
Stands dark, dusty and dull.
Strong, tall and quiet.
Bells ringing, birds singing in the sun,
Lots of arches, different sizes.
Different pictures, different carvings.
Big book cupboards and the delicate church.
Walls all rusty, Furness Abbey houses roofless
Green moss on the old wall.
Silent night.

Daniel Finch (8)
Old Hutton CE School

THE TIGER!

What's that I spot across
The way
A little tiger across the
Bay
It's eating rabbit and
Chasing deer
Oh I wish I could get near.
It seems so peaceful quiet
And calm.
Why is man hunting them
Down.
Soon they'll be gone
We'll see them no more.
How can we do it,
There should be a law.

Alexandra Kneale (8)
Our Lady Of The Rosary RC Primary School

BLACKBURN IS MY TEAM

Blackburn is the best,
They are better than the rest.
We're going to win the league,
Sherwood, Gallagher and Sutton too,
Score the goals,
All past you.
We shout and sing
And jump with joy
6-0 will do just fine.

The game is over,
We have won.
It's time for home
With smiling faces
And no voice left.
We sit in silence,
Oh what a good game.

David Woodburn (8)
Our Lady Of The Rosary RC Primary School

FOOD

Food is lovely,
Sometimes bubbly,
I hate mustard, I love custard
I love cheeseburgers and fries,
If I get them my sister cries.
I love pizza, my sister doesn't,

Then you see I like my food
Oh no! I think I'm going to be *sick!*

Lauren Langhorn (9)
Our Lady Of The Rosary RC Primary School

TEN DANCING SPACEMEN

Ten dancing spacemen dancing in a row
One falls down to earth
Then there were nine.
Nine dancing spacemen
One jumps up and was never seen again
Then there were eight.
Eight dancing spacemen
One looks at the sun and was blinded
And then there were seven.
Seven dancing spacemen
One starts jumping up
Then there were six.
Six dancing spacemen jumping up and down
One falls through the moon
Then there were five.
Five dancing spacemen
One was captured by an alien and never seen again
Then there were four.
Four dancing spacemen dancing on the moon
One thought the moon was cheese and had a slice and died
Then there were three.
Three dancing spacemen dancing in a line
One fell into a pool of chilli and drowned
Then there were two.
Two dancing spacemen dancing in a line
One took ill and had a fit and
And then there was one.
One spaceman all alone
He got in his rocket because he was bored
Then his rocket exploded and that was the end of
Him.

Laura Duffin (8)
Our Lady Of The Rosary RC Primary School

TEN DANCING ALIENS

Ten dancing aliens dancing on the moon
One fainted and then there were nine.
Nine dancing aliens invading the planet
One went back in time and then there were eight.
Eight dancing aliens playing rock and roll
One got a headache then there were seven.
Seven dancing aliens all fell in love
One got dumped then there were six.
Six dancing aliens on a boat
One got fed to the sharks then there were five.
Five dancing aliens on their bikes
One went to casualty then there were four.
Four dancing aliens all in a row
One got fed up then there were three.
Three dancing aliens skiing in the south
One caught a cold then there were two.
Two dancing aliens in the jungle
One got lost then there was one.
One dancing alien playing in the sea
A crab bit its toe then there were none!

Alyssa Greenway (8)
Our Lady Of The Rosary RC Primary School

SKY

Oh my oh my what a beautiful sky,
I love you so much I could never say bye bye,

The stars and Mars are my favourite too,
I love your colours, shades of blue.

Emma Chalker (8)
Our Lady Of The Rosary RC Primary School

NEIGHBOURS

I have a house with ten bedrooms
They have a house with two bedrooms
I have a giant water fountain
They just have a goldfish pond
I have a restaurant
They have a little kitchen
I have four TVs
They have a radio
I have a twenty-five acre garden
They have a cabbage patch
I have a taxi
They have an old banger
Now they've changed it to a sports car
How am I going to keep up with that!

Greig Hill (8)
Plumbland School

FIRE

Fire, fire burning bright,
Like a tiger of the night.
Shh! Here he comes crawling.
Not a sound he makes.
Then he pounces up,
A flames that's burning bright,
Like the tiger in the night.

Colin Sessford (9)
Plumbland School

Morning Sounds

The birds are singing
Then my dad is whistling
My dog is barking
The kettle is singing
The radio is popping
The birds are whistling
Hot tea is pouring
What can I do about
The noise?

Helen Rutherford (9)
Plumbland School

Lightning

The clouds are dark,
and lightning strikes,
like a knife.
As quick as sound
it flashes,
and strikes to ground
with a great big
crackle.

Philip Shackleton (9)
Plumbland School

GLAMOROUS GRANNY

My glamorous granny wears
a pink dress
it has
yellow polka dots on,
she wears
a red bow
in her hair
she is mad
as a mad march hare
but I
still love her.

Tom Grant (8)
Plumbland School

ORANGE

The colour of the rust on the
old ship in the harbour.
The satsuma in the fruit bowl.
The sunset on a summer night.
The sun burning hot in the sky.
My T-shirt in the drawer.
The sand in the builder's yard.
The autumn leaves rustling down the road.
The old box in the attic.
The pencil in my pencil case.

Jon Ridley (10)
Plumbland School

THE SHEEPDOG

The sheepdog is black.
The sheepdog is white
and it sleeps all night.
It chases sheep in the morning.
It chases sheep in the evening
and when the day is dawning
it starts yawning.
The shepherd's whistle is sharp
and fast, it tells the dog to
go to the right.
The shepherd's whistle is soft
and long, it tells the dog to
go to the left.
The sheepdog has great days
with the shepherd and
enjoys them all.

Calum Hill (11)
Plumbland School

RAINBOW

R ed is the burning sun
A vocado is the dewed grass
I ndigo is Sonic in a mood
N avy blue is the night sky
B lue is the deep blue ocean
O range is the sun blazing on the scorching desert
W hite is the warm milk out of the cow.

Matthew Prior (9)
Plumbland School

STARS IN THEIR EYES

Stars, stars, stars in their eyes.
Who will win? Who will lose?
Hoping and hoping over the days, hoping.
When the decision is made who has won?
I am hoping and hoping that I have won.
Here are the answers.
There's no turning back.
My best friend has won.
Have I? Oh please.
    Yes!

Angela Irving (10)
Plumbland School

THE KESTREL

Over in that gloomy tree
There lives a kestrel
It hovers over the bloodstained fields
Its eyes menacingly see something move
It dives swiftly
Its talons outstretched
As it pierces the skin
Of an unsuspecting vole
Another victim for the kestrel.

Jack Grant (10)
Plumbland School

SWALLOW'S TALE

The swallow swoops down a country lane,
Hoping not to be caught in vain.
He's looking for some tasty grub,
Not a dirty little bug.
He sits down for a short kip,
While he's looking for a sip,
Of water down by the stream,
Where the sun will always beam.
He flies along the lane once more,
Even though it's becoming a bore.
It's getting colder day by day,
The swallow will not wait at bay.
He starts to build a useless nest,
Even though he's doing his best.
But he forgets to migrate,
When he remembers it's too late.
He slowly shivers in the cold,
And forgets always to be told.
He very slowly fades away,
Never to be seen in the light of day.

Philippa Colville (10)
Raughton Head CE Primary School

Rain

Drip, drop, drip, drop,
It's raining outside.
People
Running around
Frantically
Trying to get indoors.
It looks
Cold, dull, wet and windy outside
But inside it's warm and bright.
Slam!
Someone comes in
Shutting out the wind.
Their wellies make a puddle.
Drip, drop, drip, drop,
The last drop,
To
A
Stop.

Rebecca John (11)
Raughton Head CE Primary School

Season

The winter snow glistens like drops of diamonds
but has the sting of a barbed wire.
Spring's magic makes the fluffy lambs and the
clear skies a symbol of peace.
Summer shows the fields full of poppies looking
like a wildfire.
The autumn wind brings the first signs of winter.

Dale Hedley (11)
Robert Ferguson Primary School

MY FAMILY

My mum is always shopping
My dad is on the chair
My sister's in her bedroom
What is she doing there?

I have a passion for motor bikes
My dad just sits and stares
At me with a bike book stuck in my face
We have some pet horses, both are mares.

My mum returns from shopping
I help her with the bags
Mum puts the tea on
While I stand and dance.

Carl Wills (10)
Robert Ferguson Primary School

LOOKS LIKE

The big green field looks like the
large sheet that covers my bed.
The huge white clouds look like flocks
of big white fluffy sheep.
The large blue sky looks like the blue
cold ocean that people swim in.
The small dark blackboard looks like the
massive black hole that's very scary.

Kevin Mulraine (11)
Robert Ferguson Primary School

THE SEASONS

Winter is coming to an end,
Out comes the sun.
Daffodils bloom,
Everything comes out of their hiding place.

Summer sun gleams like a ball of fire,
Holidays all around.
Beaches full of people,
Grass blowing like a carpet in a gentle breeze.

Autumn leaves fall down,
All colours have a meaning.
It gets colder,
And animals hibernate and get ready for winter.

Winter is here,
The fun has disappeared.
Morning dew like diamonds,
Trees like skeletons.

Leanne Hardon (10)
Robert Ferguson Primary School

THE COLOURFUL SEASONS

Spring is when the flowers bloom.
Summer is when the sun is blazing.
Autumn is when the colourful leaves fall.
Winter nights are long and cold.

Nicky Falder (11)
Robert Ferguson Primary School

MY FAMILY

My dad is in the front room,
He is watching telly,
Sitting there with his beer,
And his feet so smelly.

My mam is in the kitchen,
Making a big cake.
She also likes reading,
But I think she'd rather bake.

My sister is up in her room,
Homework - lots to do,
Next year when I'm at Morton,
I might have lots too.

My dog is in the back room,
Curled up in her bed,
She is fast asleep now,
But she'll wake when she gets fed.

I am just in my room,
On the computer I like to play,
And if no one calls me,
I'll stay here all day.

Well that is all my family,
Everyone I've done,
I know we are not many,
But we still have lots of fun.

Jack Guyan (10)
Robert Ferguson Primary School

THE OPEN DOOR

I open the door
I see a road with no end
Yellowness of the desert
And an old car jogging up the road

I open the door
I see a fair
Shouting of the children
And a big wheel squeaking as it goes round

I open the door
I see a carnival
Colours of their magical clothing
And loud music pumping through my ears.

Hannah Stephenson (11)
Robert Ferguson Primary School

MY FAMILY

My dad is watching sport
My mam is cleaning
I am drawing a picture
My sister is reading.

My cousins are playing
Riding on their bikes
My auntie is listening to the radio
My uncle likes going for hikes.

Rachel Bulman (10)
Robert Ferguson Primary School

SEASONS

In spring the newly born hop around with glee.
The deer eating grass from the meadow
And enjoying every blade.

In summer the beautiful red sun setting behind the hills.
The long days and short nights coming and going.

In autumn the golden leaves fall from
Their hiding place in the branches,
Floating down, down like a balloon with little air.

The winter snow glistening like sparkling glass.
The gusting wind screaming like a banshee.

Michael Handford (10)
Robert Ferguson Primary School

VICTORY FOR A SOLDIER

The soldier waits on the rough, green grass of the battle ground,
Waiting for his enemy,
Up walks a scruffy man,
Drawing his sword from his scabbard.
The soldier makes a snap,
Very quick and spry.
The enemy loses his head,
And it's 'Victory for a soldier'.

Stacey Brown (11)
Robert Ferguson Primary School

HALLOWE'EN

Horrifying hallowe'en,
All the ghosts come out to be seen.
Lank and scary with blazing eyes,
Look out, look out for a big surprise.
Open the door if you dare,
Witches and zombies could be there.
Everything's scary, everything's dark.
Eek! Was that a werewolf bark?
No, it was just my imagination.

Cristie Lynnette Millican (11)
Robert Ferguson Primary School

SEASONS

Winter is a time for snow
The ice is glistening with a glow.
The snow is flying everywhere
Over the ground and in the air.
The summer comes, the grass turns green
As green as anyone has ever seen.
The autumn arrives, the leaves all drop
They hit the water with a plop.
The spring is near, the people know
Flowers change and forests grow.

Scott Davidson (11)
Robert Ferguson Primary School

4 SEASONS

Autumn

Leaves, leaves fall to the ground.
All the birds are Africa bound.
The blazing sun turns red.
Cold nights start when I'm in my bed.

> *Winter*
>
> Sledging, sledging down a hill.
> Lots of snow on a window-sill.
> Snowmen building and snowball fights.
> Don't forget the pretty Christmas lights.

Spring

Cold days begin to get very few.
All the glistening morning dew.
The baby lambs all newly born.
Yellow and red are the colours that make a lovely dawn.

> *Summer*
>
> Summer always has a burning sun.
> Hot days are so much fun.
> Hooray, no school.
> Now I can go swimming in a pool.

John Blenkharn (11)
Robert Ferguson Primary School

THE TIGER

The tiger, eminence of the jungle.
His coat, his pride, that lets him hide
Among the long, tall grass.
He sights his victim who is unknown to its fate,
Then on he creeps with the stealth of a thief.
A tempest grows inside his mind
Then it springs onto the woeful animals behind.
Panic brews in the zebra's hooves,
It kicks and it struggles
Though resistance is futile.
The teeth sink in and the pain increases
The zebra deceases
Becoming the tiger's prey.

Luke Haslett (11)
St Begh's Junior School, Whitehaven

SMOOTHLY, SWIFTLY . . .

Smoothly, swiftly across the sand,
Slowly, slimy on the desert land,
To and fro,
It will go,
Sliding here and sliding there,
It's a snake you know.

Smoothly, swiftly in the burning sun,
If you see one - run, run, run!

Kimberley Elliott (10)
St Begh's Junior School, Whitehaven

AUTUMN

I love being in the country
when autumn's in the air
leaves crispy, crunching like a
crinoline dress
as we walk without a care.

The colours are changing into brown,
yellow then red
until they tumble helplessly to the ground
The temperature's calming, cool and crisp
for autumn is in the air.

Lauren Shimmin (11)
St Begh's Junior School, Whitehaven

THE LIONESS

Stalking your prey through the long camouflaging grass,
Sleek as a snake and strong as the wind,
Stealthily you creep through African jungles,
Waiting to pounce,
On an innocent gazelle,
For cubs
Are awaiting lunch,
Pounce!
What's for dessert?

Jordan Wells (10)
St Begh's Junior School, Whitehaven

THE MAGICAL COUNTRYSIDE

I walk gently through the long, sweet, green grass,
The harsh sun warming my face,
The cool breeze blowing against my beaming cheeks.
I feel as light as floating feathers.
I feel as happy as three giggling, gurgling babies put together.
The beautiful flowers tickle my bare feet as I tread by.
Ahead I find a flowing river,
Blue and sparkling, like something out of a fairy tale.
The sun makes little diamonds appear
Which hypnotise me into a soft, weary dream.

Jessica Thompson (11)
St Begh's Junior School, Whitehaven

A GARDEN OF BEAUTY

Daffodils and tulips grow so very tall,
Primroses and pansies stay small,
Blossoms in the garden make me smile,
My favourite one of all is the red rose on my window-sill.

The trees in my garden are all shades of green.
They must be the nicest I've ever seen,
The horse chestnuts brings children from all around.
To gather the conkers that lie on the ground.

Stephanie Parkinson (10)
St Begh's Junior School, Whitehaven

SHOOTING STARS

Shooting stars leave glittery trails,
Like the tears of weeping snails.
Meteorites leave great destruction,
And who is there to do the construction?
Is there really life on Mars?
Do Martians drive little green cars?
Spaceships fly through the galaxy.
If I were on board I'd shout
      W
       H
        E
         E
          E
           E
            E
             E
              !

Stephanie Woodward (10)
St Cuthbert's RC School, Windermere

SPACE

Space is colourful
Space is bright
Space is everything
Space is night.

Ross Santamera (10)
St Cuthbert's RC School, Windermere

A Little Star

It shines so bright,
Clear as the night,
A little, little, little star,
Up so far,
Bright like we are,
A little,
    Little,
        Little,
            Little,
                Star.

Justin Pape (11)
St Cuthbert's RC School, Windermere

I'm Thinking Of A Place

I'm thinking of a place, a very dark place,
Where could it be, but the one and only space.
I'm travelling through - but what to do?
Just to see the sun, Jupiter and the moon.
What fascinating sights,
Some very bright lights,
But some are very dim,
But I wonder what lies within.

Sam Cleghorn (11)
St Cuthbert's RC School, Windermere

FUDGE THE GORILLA

Fudge is a gorilla,
Soft and cuddly,
Fudge is a gorilla,
Cute as could be,
Fudge is a gorilla,
Toffee the teddy sits on his lap,
Fudge is a gorilla,
He is dark brown,
Fudge is a gorilla,
With light brown paws and face.
Fudge is a gorilla,
He's having a race!

Kate Buxton (11)
St Margaret's CE Primary School, Durham City

MY BEST FRIEND

She's as skinny as a stick
She's always got a trick
Her sense of humour is great
Except the joke about the plate!
She wears designer clothes
She *always* loves to pose
Girl power's her fave
She's really cool and brave
The boys think she's gorge
You've guessed it, it's George.

Emily Ashfield (10)
St Margaret's CE Primary School, Durham City

THE DEATH OF MY GRANDAD!

The death of my grandad came as such a shock,
My heart just stopped beating like the hands moving round a clock.
I couldn't eat or drink,
I couldn't cry or think.
I didn't know what to do.

The good times we had were such fun,
Once we went to the beach and lay under the sun.
I'm pleased I can remember the good things we've done.
Now all I can do is think about the good times we had.
And whatever happens, I still love my grandad.

Rachael Stewart (10)
St Margaret's CE Primary School, Durham City

I WANT TO BE ILL

I want to be ill.
My friend is.
The teacher likes her but never lets me go home.
My mum said 'Tell your teacher then,' but she still won't.
I want to be ill.
A few months later my friend died in a car crash.
Going to the hospital and she said 'I wish I wasn't ill,
I wish I wasn't here.'
And she still haunts her home and me and
She says 'I wish I wasn't dead.'
I wish, I wish, I wish,
It's all gone dead.

Joy Rathbone (11)
St Margaret's CE Primary School, Durham City

DOWN THE GREEN PATHS OF THE FOREST

Down the green paths of the forest
The striking tiger prowled,
From the distant trees just within his gaze
There came a mighty howl.

The wolf was there, lost and lone,
With no one to care for him,
Because when he was young his guardians died,
And no others to him came.

Perhaps the wolf's opposite
Is the baby rabbit, safe and sound,
In his cosy home with his mother,
His snug little compound.

The adder, silent and sinister,
Slowly sneaks through the forest floor,
A little mouse once lived there,
But when the adder came, he lived no more.

Everything in the forest
Has to sometimes be cruel to survive,
If not, nothing in the forest
Would ever stay alive.

But the forest isn't all doom and gloom,
Some parts are happy and good;
Like the bees buzzing among the trees
And the fresh sweet smelling wood.

Leila Panesar (10)
St Margaret's CE Primary School, Durham City

LITTLE BOY MONDAY

Mum, please let me stay at home,
My teacher, he won't mind,
I promised I would go to school,
If only the sun would shine,
I don't have very many friends,
I have nothing to play.
My school life is dull, not one day, but every day.
My teacher, well, to say the least, he's a little dull,
But now, it's worst, 'cos he's gone on holiday to Hull.
Please don't make me go to school today,
Don't worry son, it is only Sunday.

Shanaka Kahakachchi (11)
St Margaret's CE Primary School, Durham City

THE MUSTY OLD KEY

As I remove the rusty old key from its hook
and slot it into the keyhole for the last time,
I smell the musty smell for the last time,
and hear the jangle of the key locking the old, wooden door.
And as I stroll back with it, I feel the sharp dents in it
and smell the old, musty smell.
For as long as I live, I shall remember the cold, rough touch
of the tarnished, battered, old key.

Rebecca J C Lancelot (11)
St Margaret's CE Primary School, Durham City

THE TANK

It rumbles slowly through the streets,
Its destination uncertain,
To glorious victories in battle?
No, more like a crater for its grave
While soldiers around it shout,
Cries of victory? Screams of defeat?
Both probably, though it'll never know,
It and its crew forgotten,
While heroes, smart-clothed, receive shining medals,
It will lie there in smoke and mud,
But now around it civilians cheer,
As it plods slowly through the city,
Filling the air with an acrid smell,
Its crew remembering the old lie
Dulce et decorum est pro patria mori,
But dying for one's country,
Is the same as dying for nothing.

Jonathan Gordon Best (10)
St Margaret's CE Primary School, Durham City

A GIANT'S LUNCH BOX

The box itself is as big as a
suitcase and is as clear as glass.
There is . . . sandwiches as large as a cornfield,
a biscuit as round as the sun, some crisps
as crunchy as ice and a drink that swirls
like the ocean and a drumstick as greasy as a pole.

Louisa Kate Dobson (10)
St Margaret's CE Primary School, Durham City

The Fox Hunt

'Baloo, Haloo!' the horn sounds.
To all the horses and the hounds.
A frightened fox appears ahead.
A shot rings out, then all is dead . . .

Katie Yeats (11)
St Margaret's CE Primary School, Durham City

The Monster Underground

Deep, deep under the ground
Underneath the oak we found
It lurks itself under the tree
Watching out for you and me
It looks for its prey lurking ahead
It jumps upon them then all is dead.

Lizzie Thomson (11)
St Margaret's CE Primary School, Durham City

Easter Eggs

I am very excited, I just cannot wait for Easter,
When I get that lovely chocolate egg with my name upon it,
Just a hollow chocolate egg with a surprise in the middle,
But I have a long time to wait because it is only the 16th of September.

Sophie Dobson (10)
St Margaret's CE Primary School, Durham City

FRED THE FROG

Last week I met a frog called Fred.
His friendly face is sweet and cute,
His webbed feet couldn't fit in a boot,
I don't think he'd ever cry,
His goggly eyes are far too dry.
If he was lost he'd never be found,
When he moves he doesn't make a sound.
His elegant leap lands him safely on the ground,
Away from creatures that prey on him.
Flickering, his tongue reaches out to catch his lunch,
Then he makes himself comfy and rests on a bunch of leaves.
So now he's asleep, not to be disturbed and
I'm going now I hope he hasn't heard!

Priya Prasad (11)
St Margaret's CE Primary School, Durham City

THE STAFF ROOM

Cigarette butts litter the floor,
New ones still half lit,
Old ones crisp and dry with muddy footprints trodden into them.
There are beer cans still half full,
Some still since last Tuesday,
When the school burnt down 'cause of Mr Laidler's last cigarette,
No more loud guffaws and huge burps will come
From down in the depths of a kid's worst nightmare
The staff room.

Charlotte Hutchinson (11)
St Margaret's CE Primary School, Durham City

It's My Birthday In A Minute

'It's my birthday in a minute'
My little sister said
She always says it every day
As soon as she's got out of bed

She asks for presents
For teddies and a ball
She shouts 'It's my birthday'
While running down the hall

'It's my birthday in a minute'
My little sister said
She always says it every night
Before she goes to bed.

Elizabeth Southgate (11)
St Margaret's CE Primary School, Durham City

Two Cuddly Dogs

Two cuddly dogs,
Sat side to side,
They both lived in a fairground,
So they got a free ride.

They wandered round the fairground,
They walked round and round,
The two dogs had a very good time,
And then they made this rhyme!

Julia Robson (11)
St Margaret's CE Primary School, Durham City

THE LITTLE LOST SOUL

The sky was black as jet,
No one had left the old house yet,
The people who entered never came back,
Rumour has it, they're long since dead.
But still, she wanders the corridors like a little lost soul,
The little ghost of Emma Jane wanders all alone.
Her lonely voice whispers 'Children please come out,
Please come out and play with me, please come out and play.'
It echoes through the empty rooms and up the chimney spout.
But the little ghost of Emma Jane will never see a child about.
They'd all been told by their mums and dads to keep away from there.
They'd been told that they'll die a horrible death if to go there,
they'd ever dare.
Emma Jane, a little lost soul.
Emma Jane, she wanders all alone.

Ami Sawran-Smith (11)
St Margaret's CE Primary School, Durham City

SEAWEED

Seaweed, seaweed it's what I like best.
Seaweed, seaweed it's slippery and wet.
But what I like best of all about seaweed
is that it's like the colour of dark,
wet oak leaves glinting in the moonlight.
Sometimes it's cold, sometimes it's not,
but I don't care because it's my seaweed.

Joanne Weeding (10)
St Margaret's CE Primary School, Durham City

THE STAFF ROOM

Smoke rises and swearing and laughter fills the air.
Fag ends and empty beer cans litter the floor.
Half eaten pizzas in their boxes.
Teachers talking about evil pupils out to play.
Graffiti all over the walls.
A dark, towering shadow fixed in the doorway.
The dreaded teacher enters . . . silence.

Will Evans (10)
St Margaret's CE Primary School, Durham City

WHAT I THINK ABOUT WAR

What I feel about war,
I will tell you,
I think it's about greediness, cruelness and hate,
All those soldiers dead for nothing,
Except land, money and gold.

What I feel about war,
I'll tell you,
All the fields full of blood,
All the bombs that blow up people,
It is unnecessary for those wars.

All the families waiting,
Waiting for their heroes to return,
But when they think they're going to come back,
They never do,
How cruel is war?

Aysha Rafique (11)
St Monica's Preparatory School, Carlisle

WISHES

If I could wish,
I'd be a fish and swim in the ocean blue.

I'd jump and splash like a flash.
I'd swim and swim and swim,
Until I was thin.

I'd jump up and down
Until I nearly drown,
Oh what fun it would be.

If I got hungry I'd eat a quiche
While looking at a dog on a leash
And I can jump up and down.

Then the fishermen come
Oh no, oh no!
It's time to be caught.

I quickly swim,
I can't get away,
I'm stuck.

I'm going to be caught,
Sold on to the market,
Oh, I so do wish I was me.

I'm going to be dead fish in a dish
Skinned and eaten
In a dash.

All is left is my bones,
Nice and fine,
I have resigned.

Oh why me?
I never ate fish,
I wouldn't hurt them.

Yasemin Padidar-Nazar (10)
St Monica's Preparatory School, Carlisle

THE TRAIN

Chickety poo!
Chickety poo!
Chickety, chickety, chickety poo!
The train is on the run!
The train is on the run!
He's off to California!
He's off to California!
Chickety poo!
Chickety poo!
Chickety, chickety, chickety poo!
Where's he gone to now?
Where's he gone to now?
Is he over the hill?
Is he under the bridge?
Is he past the crossing?
Is he still on his route?
Chickety poo!
Chickety poo!
Chickety, chickety, chickety poo!

Sarah Colquhoun (10)
St Monica's Preparatory School, Carlisle

BIRTHDAY WAITING

When my birthday's really near,
I will give a great big cheer.
Ten days to go!
Much more exciting than snow.
Nine days, eight days,
Waiting's such a drool,
But much more exciting than school.
Seven days of waiting,
The time is slow to pass,
I hope I don't get a new door
That would be such a bore.
Six days, five days all to wait,
I'll go and swing the gate.
Four days left,
Maybe I will get a new pet,
A dog, a pony?
No such luck!
I'll probably be given a rubber duck.
Three days, two days,
I cannot wait.
One day, finished.
No more waiting.
Presents 1, 2, 3.
I'll go out and open them under a tree.
A skateboard, rollerblades,
Oh so cool,
Definitely this is better than school.

Aoife Kieran (10)
St Monica's Preparatory School, Carlisle

MY DOG

My dog is very lazy
And he sleeps all day.
He is very old and he is also bold.
I love my cuddly dog.

My dog is very wide,
And he is full of pride.
I take him for walks, he likes it.
He always ends up in the dike.

I play with him a lot.
I comb him nearly every day.
He likes it in a funny way.
I love my dog.

Pippa Stobart (11)
St Monica's Preparatory School, Carlisle

RAIN

I hear pit-a-pat on the window-pane
Oh yes, could it be rain?
Oh no, it's only the dog scratching on the window-pane.

What do I hear now, pit-a-pat on the roof tops?
It's rain, it's rain, oh yes it's rain.
I love the rain, especially when it runs off onto the window-pane.

I like splashing in all the puddles,
The water goes up so high,
And I always get splashed in my eye.

Sarah MacDowall (9)
St Monica's Preparatory School, Carlisle

TIGERS

Tigers can be so sweet and nice
Yet they can be oh so fearsome.
Tigers have a way of life,
That is by killing creatures.

Oh, poor little boar
Or even the buffalo,
Who fell under his mighty gaze,
Will soon become his meal for today.

When, at last they have eaten well
They go back to their little dell.
Then they fall asleep and dream
Of little baby buffaloes.

When they awake, they see a snake,
But they're not even scared of tarantulas.
When they eat a snake, it's their kind of cake
And little baby buffalo.

Sarah Frost (10)
St Monica's Preparatory School, Carlisle

OF YOU BEFORE YOU DIED

I look up to the north sky,
And shining there is your star.
I feel as though you are near me,
Even though heaven is so far.

I wonder why it happened,
This isn't the first time I've cried.
I keep seeing illusions of you,
Of you before you died.

I look at your picture,
Still there in its frame.
Every time I do something else,
My head echoes your name.

I keep thinking about it,
Why did it have to be you?
I suppose God wanted you up there,
But why does it have to be true?

Carolyn Koussa (11)
St Monica's Preparatory School, Carlisle

MY FUNNY PETS

I have a cat, fluffy and soft,
She never leaves my side.

I also have a kitten small,
He is always playful.

I have a dog, thin and keen,
He so often barks at me.

There are five cuddly puppies,
They are my mummy's.

I have got a grey mouse,
That runs about the house.

My hamster lives in a cage,
He's always happy, never in a rage.

My pets include a horse and a cow,
Which leaves me no time when I can browse.

Robert Swindells (9)
St Monica's Preparatory School, Carlisle

THE RACING CAR

I am a racing car, off I go.
Around the corner as I pass,
faster and faster past a car
I come roaring into the pits.
They change my tyres and my wing.
Out I go past the line.
One more lap as I go.
Around the corner one more time,
swerving and sliding like I'm skating.
My V10 engine roaring like a train.
'I have won, I have won.
I have won first place'
I say to myself.
My car has served me well.

Ben Smith (10)
St Monica's Preparatory School, Carlisle

SNOOKER

Let's have a game of snooker,
Send the red off to bed,
Pot the black into the sack,
Get the green off the scene,
Drop the brown all the way down,
Send the blue to Timbuktu.
Put the pink down the sink,
Bellow the yellow into the pocket,
And throw the white into the night.
All the colours have gone away,
I hope they'll come back another day.

Richard Blacklock (10)
St Monica's Preparatory School, Carlisle

SCHOOL

Each day when I come to school,
The teacher comes in soon after,
He'll make us all do work,
And then it's a place for no laughter.

First we say prayers and then go back to class,
Then we do English, geography and maths,
For the rest of the morning we work really hard,
And then we come in class, and do more tasks.

We'd work till five to twelve,
And then we go to lunch,
We say prayers before we sit down,
And then we eat, crunch, crunch.

Stephen Harris (10)
St Monica's Preparatory School, Carlisle

RAIN IS A PAIN

I like watching the rain
Falling down on the window-pane.
You jump in all the puddles
And get wet again.
You have to be insane
To go in the rain,
The rain is a pain
Unless you're insane.
Do you think rain is a pain?
It's not as nice as a horse's mane.
When it rains I use my umbrella,
It is yellow.

Georgina Cregan (9)
St Monica's Preparatory School, Carlisle

A Rainy Day

Swish, slosh goes the rain,
Plip, plop on the window-pane,
Ruff, woof goes my Great Dane,
He wants to go on a walk again.

Munch lunch but it's still pouring,
Boo-hoo, I want to be at the zoo,
With a lion roaring,
The sun is coming out, woo-hoo.

Red, blue, lovely bright colours,
Yellow, purple colours of my salt cellars,
Orange, violet fruits and flowers,
The unicorn's gold gives me powers.

Clare Sevar (10)
St Monica's Preparatory School, Carlisle

My Special Pets

I have lots of pets,
I have a mouse squeaking round the house,
I have a mole and it lives in a hole.

I have a fish it lives in my dish,
I have some dogs and they live in a bog,
I have a pig and it is very big.

I have a cat and it sleeps on my mat,
I have a bear and it's in my care,
I have a frog and I call it Sprog.

They are all my very special funny pets.

Victoria Milbourn (8)
St Monica's Preparatory School, Carlisle

THAT DARN CAT

I've got a cat called DC
Every time I go to town
He jumps out of the window
Once he did and
My mum nearly crashed.

It was time for tea
But he never comes
And at 8.00
He jumps out of the window

And at night when
I am asleep
He jumps onto my bed.

He made me scream last night.

Emma Sims (8)
St Monica's Preparatory School, Carlisle

BIRDS

A little bird in the sky can fly around the world
It does not need an aeroplane or a ticket to Brazil
It goes all by itself under its own power
It never needs an engine or motor power.

It can fly in any weather, whether wet or sunny
It has wings and eyes and can be very chummy
Nobody needs to control it
For it knows the way
It does not need a map or directions for its stay.

Jacqueline Haslam (9)
St Monica's Preparatory School, Carlisle

FLYING

Flying high up in the sky
In the sky, oh I wish I could fly
This sky seems so high for me to try
There is no chance for me to fly.

I wish I could fly like a bird
Through the sky, over the seas
In the places hard to see
But the sky is too high for me to try.

If I was in the sky
I would fly with great might
To see the great sights
But the sky is too high for me to try.

Sophie Robson (10)
St Monica's Preparatory School, Carlisle

FIRE, FIRE

Fire, fire it burns like mad.
Sparks go up in the air.
The colours are green, red, orange, yellow, brown and blue.
You can get burnt.
When the fire is finished the people are sad.
All you see are the ashes.
Fire, fire burning bright on bonfire night.
All the children shouting out loud.
Fire, fire it burns like mad.
See the flames blazing everywhere.
Then the fire goes out.

Rachael Fletcher (10)
St Monica's Preparatory School, Carlisle

SPACE

At night I lie and wonder,
What is up there?
I know there is Venus, Mars, lightning and thunder.

If I sent up a rocket it would just hit the stars,
And if it goes far enough it will just knock Mars.

If the Earth takes twenty-four hours to orbit,
Pluto must take longer, if not it's much stronger.

Space is so big,
Earth is so small,
Why can't Earth be tall,
Not small?

Jack Stamper (9)
St Monica's Preparatory School, Carlisle

THE FLYING MACHINE

If everyone had a flying machine
They would fly about all day
Pushing lever and switching a switch
And taking off to play

I will take to the air
Dodging a plane and skimming a tower
Swooping around with no real care
And doing it all in one hour

I'll have to make sure I don't run out of fuel
'Cos I'll crash to the ground and explode
My machine will only run up in mid-air
It refuses to go on the road.

Jamie Benzie (10)
St Monica's Preparatory School, Carlisle

SIMBA MY KITTEN

Simba my kitten, loves to pounce,
One day guess - yes he caught a mouse.
He loves playing catch all over the house.

I have two more kittens, one is called Frittens,
She likes to play with my sister's mittens
Her favourite food is a slice of chicken.

My other kitten is called Mr Chivers,
For a dainty morsel he eats livers
Which gives all of us shivers.

At the end of the day they go to sleep,
And from then till next morning there's not a peep.
Then they play with the Duplo, then they are asleep.

Geoffrey Smith (9)
St Monica's Preparatory School, Carlisle

I REALLY WOULD LIKE

Mum, I really would like,
A small water sprite,
Or what about a kangaroo,
You could buy one from the zoo!

Okay, what about a bike?
I could put my little sprite
In the pocket
Of my bike.

And I'm sure my kangaroo
Which comes from the zoo
Will help you!

So please
Could you
Immediately
Go to the zoo.

Katherine Lynch (8)
St Monica's Preparatory School, Carlisle

LAST NIGHT

One night before I went to sleep
I found myself counting sheep.
When I was up to thirty-three
I heard a scream, boom, tweedle-dee.

At first I thought it was a monster,
It didn't sound like my sister's hamster.
Then I heard a tweet, tweet, ouch,
I looked, it's not coming from the couch.

It sounded a little like a mouse,
But we don't have them in our house.
All quiet, then a tweet, tweet, jerk,
This sounded as if someone was hurt.

The tweet, tweet, jerk went on for an age,
I soon discovered it came from budgie's cage.
I pulled off the cover and ouch, ouch, ping,
My poor little budgie had fallen off his swing.

Louise Irving (8)
St Monica's Preparatory School, Carlisle

CROCODILE

I have a little crocodile -
He's only twelve feet long.
He never has a smily face
Because he's always wrong.

His teeth are sharp as carving knives
Just right for eating meat.
He snaps at folk he doesn't like -
He bit off auntie's feet!

I need him put on rations
'Cos he's getting rather fat.
I'll make him eat tomatoes
But he'll have to pay for that!

Jodie Parkhouse (10)
St Monica's Preparatory School, Carlisle

MY TOYS

Last Thursday in my bedroom
I heard a big boom!
I saw my toys alive, including my teddy, Clive
Am I dead or am I alive?

I went running to tell my mum
She said she would get out of bed and come.
When my mum got to my room she said:
'I bet that was you acting cool
No I take that back, I bet that was you
Acting like a fool.'

Shardia Sahib (9)
St Monica's Preparatory School, Carlisle

My Fantasy

As I lay upon the lush, green grass,
the warm sunshine gleams over me.
I sit well tucked into a book full of adventure and excitement.
Knights and dragons fight, princesses cry for help
as they lean over their tower windows,
evil witches stir magic potions in their black cauldrons
kings and queens, and knights are brave and fearless soldiers.
I read for hours not taking a glance at anything elsewhere.
Birds whistle sweet and glorious melodies in their trees.
The cat next door sits on the garden wall,
it stares as if to say 'What are you doing?'
but eventually he gets bored and walks away.
The air gets colder, it's hard to see
as the sun is nearly gone.
I feel my eyes getting weaker.
I close the book and stroll inside the house.
The fantasy has darkened.

Ellen Mattinson (11)
Trinity CE Junior School

Space

Planets are red
The galaxy blue
The Milky Way's white
And spacemen are too.

The Earth is round
Spaceships are square
Asteroids are rectangular
And black holes aren't there.

Matthew Carter (10)
Trinity CE Junior School

HIPPIES!

We love trees!
We hug trees!
We have dreadlocks in
Our hair
We sing around camp-fires
Humming and strumming
Guitars.
Our clothes are pretty weird,
Our tastes are
Very strange.
Flares, waistcoats,
Bright colours.
Dreadlocks a mile long.
We wear stilettos
A mile high.
So high we
Touch the sky.
But for now,
Peace man!

Hetty Partington (11)
Trinity CE Junior School

FOUR WHITE SKELETONS IN THE SEA

Four white skeletons in the sea
No one knows except for me
The treasure chest that was theirs
The treasure is my bed
I am the eel that lives down there
So go away or you will pay
OK.

Adrian J Read (10)
Trinity CE Junior School

LITTLE MR ALIEN

Sitting up in space,
I have always wondered
What had happened to your face
You can be so happy,
You can be so sad,
But I have always wondered
Why you're just so mad!
You can live on Pluto,
You can live on Mars,
You can live on Jupiter,
But you can't live on the stars!

Jonathan E Branthwaite (10)
Trinity CE Junior School

MOTHER'S DAY

Mothers that are loving
Mothers that are caring
Mothers that have babies
Must all be ladies.

My mother I love you so much
You're the best thing I've ever touched (hug)
You say a lot of sweet things
And I like it when you sing.
So keep on being caring and loving
And no more shoving.

Lots of love, kisses and hugs.

Deborah Paris (11)
Trinity CE Junior School

UFO

I see you dashing
Flashing high above
Flickering beyond the stars
Further, further away than Mars
As I wonder
When I'm in bed
Are you alive or are you dead
I wonder, I wonder . . .

Robert MacKereth (10)
Trinity CE Junior School

CANADA GOOSE

She glides through the air
with the greatest of ease,
her wings do not tire of surfing
the breeze.
They fold up like those of a plane
and then stretch out to the side
again.
On and on like this she flies
endlessly without missing a beat.

Katie Green (11)
Trinity CE Junior School

PLANETS

Planets are blue
Planets are green
Planets are purple
Planets are yellow
Planets are red
Planets are spotty
Planets are blotty
Planets are pink
Planets are orange
Planets are big
Planets are small
Planets have rings
Planets are weird.

Peter Scott (11)
Trinity CE Junior School

CHOCOLATE CHEEKS

At school a boy called John has chubby little cheeks.
He's mean and not clean.
His mouth is covered in chocolate
And his hands, of chocolate melted in his pockets.
In his mouth his teeth are yellow-green, a mouldy browny.
His face is covered with spots and dots.
He's a greedy machine.

Rachel Fox (11)
Trinity CE Junior School

WORDS

Words talk
They get crossed out
They come out of your mouth
They are written out on paper
They're gone.

Hannah Moore (9)
Vickerstown School

MAGIC TURKISH DELIGHT

Incredible, silk
Outstanding, enchanting, cool
Melting, tasty warm.

Alison Knight (10)
Wensleydale Middle School

TURKISH DELIGHT

Magical juices
Delightful sudden fragrances
Enchanting smells.

Amy Hutchinson (10)
Wensleydale Middle School

What Is Mercury?

Mercury is a piece of silver paper
shining in the air.

A ten pence piece glowing,
but slowly getting dim.

Mercury is a white cylinder
in a dark black tunnel.

A burning pearl, heated by fire
in a black cupboard.

Mercury is a grey dot, floating round
in an everlasting bin liner.

Nicola Cherkassky (10)
Wensleydale Middle School

What Is Saturn?

Saturn is a ringed doughnut in the night sky.
Saturn is a scoop of vanilla tossed in a mouth of blackness.
Saturn is a large Frisbee in a black sheet.
It is a round pebble floating in a black sea of pearls.
Saturn is a ball of ice in a sack of coal.
Saturn is a yellow football ringed with
Thousands of coloured Slinkeys.

Lance Allen (10) & David Jagger (11)
Wensleydale Middle School

THE GREEN DRAGON

Gathering speed goes the Green Dragon,
Grimy smoke grows from its gaping nostrils
It's a giant gargantuan monster travelling along.
It enters a gaping great tunnel
and gives an ear-splitting whistle
Glowing eyes gleam on with glistening
glossiness.
Gathering speed it gets faster and faster,
and grinds to a halt.
Gaily dressed people alight the train.
The gaudy Green Dragon
I'm home once again.

Christopher Campbell (11)
Wensleydale Middle School

THE TRAIN

The train master blows and off it goes,
Further and further down the track
Faster and faster fleeing fearlessly flying
like a cheetah.
Racing and storming like a dragon,
Steaming through the tunnel faster than ever.
Its lights gleaming like a sparkling
firework,
Never going out.

Craig Martin (10)
Wensleydale Middle School

A Dolphin

Gliding through the wide deep ocean,
Like an elephant on army green land.

In and out of waves,
Like a monkey on dark brown branches.
Swinging from tree to tree,
Branch to branch, leaf to leaf.

Waving my elegant tail in the glistening sun,
Like ducks jumping in and out of a bulrush pond
Splashing the soily earth.

Singing, singing with my wailing noise,
Desperate to be played with.
Waiting in the water's destiny,
Wagging my nose like a seal with a bouncing ball.

The sky peels open, coatings of black air,
Grey clouds of dusk setting in the sky.
I wave goodbye with my fin in the air,
Waving, to darkness, with saddening despair.

Laura Watson (10)
Wensleydale Middle School

Narnia's Woods

Fantastic crisp snow
Bitter flaking winter air,
Breezy soundless wood.

Jennifer Tait (10)
Wensleydale Middle School

MONKEYS

Monkeys swinging in the trees,
Like children with a big space to play in,
Oohing ahhing, swatting the bees
Climbing in the trees.

Climbing higher, higher,
Like spiders trying to get away from water,
Arms reaching,
Legs swinging,
Climbing as high as they can.

They swing,
They climb,
They reach as high as they can . . .

Rachel Aspinall (10)
Wensleydale Middle School

THE WRINKLED OLD RHINO

His wrinkled old coat shines in the gleaming sun.
While he lazes under a palm tree,
He holds his head up proud.
Striding through the jungle,
Knocking down trees as he passes.
Roaming through the undergrowth from
Sunset till dawn,
In search of a friend.

Caroline Elsey (10)
Wensleydale Middle School

THE TRAIN POEM

The ZX13 speeding down the track,
Hear the carriages clickety clack.
As the signal moves from higher to lower.
It slams on the brakes and starts to get slower.
Through the mist it reappears,
Settling in at the platform rear.

Ross Wallis (10)
Wensleydale Middle School

THE SUN

My name is colour
I'm as old as time
From the outer reaches of the universe
I come for peace
I am very warm
and I will lighten up your day
My friends are the universe.

Stephen Pape (11)
Wensleydale Middle School

DRAGON EXPRESS

Glaring, gleaming, rushing by,
Gushing past, just like a whirlwind.
With its great booming and puffing of smoke,
You almost feel trapped.
Joined by its grand, glowing carriages
The track grumbles when it passes by
Back the train goes into the great darkness.

Nicholas Turner (11)
Wensleydale Middle School

PUFFING STEAMING DRAGON

Shiny, glossy, gleaming dragon,
Swiftly swaying side to side,
Roaring puffing steaming onwards,
Always leaning left and right,
Gusty, breezy, windy, swishy,

The crawling caterpillar begins to creep,
Burning, boiling the coal crackling,
Flying magic fills the air
Its flexible body stretches round the corner.
Its gleaming lights and its tooting horn
Screeches.
Steamy and stuffy at the station it stops.

Alison Leese (10)
Wensleydale Middle School

THE FLYING SCOTSMAN

Faster and faster,
Flowing like a river.
Further and further,
Fearlessly fleeting.
Flying down the track,
Furnace flaming hot.
Feeling scared,
Foaming furiously,
Flumes of steam.
Flying Scotsman
Flies through the night.

James Banks (11)
Wensleydale Middle School

THE ENCHANTED LION

Scheming treacherous lion,
who roars with such anger
He roams the jungle in search of
something completely magical.
His coat golden and sparkling,
rippling in the sun.
His ears turns slowly to listen to,
something completely enchanting
and exciting.

Becky Fawcus (11)
Wensleydale Middle School

WATER

My name is life,
I am as old as the world's beginning.
I am from the countryside,
Life on earth depends on me,
I am made of liquid,
I like to flow around the world.
My family is everyone.
I'll be your friend.

Cara-Jade Johnson (10)
Wensleydale Middle School

COSMIC

Have you seen my brother?
I hope you have not,
He thinks he explores space,
And all that lot.

One day he told
A complete stranger,
When he grows up,
He will be a space ranger.

Yelled he to my mum,
Screamed he to me
'Big Ben (the bully)
Is the baddy.'

Downstairs he came,
One afternoon
Shouted he to me,
'Big Ben is conquering the moon!'

He said to my mum,
'I must go there,'
But Mum refused,
To his despair.

'I'm sorry Michael,
No you don't
Not till your room is tidy.
You won't!'

Matthew Higgins (10)
Yarlside School

COSMIC

I took a trip to
Mars the other day,
but the enormous moon stood in my way.
I eventually made my way past the moon
when I was zooming round on my magic spoon.

I bounced on to Mars where the floor is so red,
and the orange clouds whizzed round my head.
The sky is very, very dark pink,
and the air is as warm as a burning ice rink.
Then my mother came outside and shouted,
Stop daydreaming!

Rachael Crewdson (11)
Yarlside School

COSMIC

I'm racing through space
At a million miles an hour.
Supersonic power.
Whizzing through the stars
I came face to face with Mars.
Like a space ranger facing danger
In my super-duper UFO,
I wondered where I should go.
Just then I woke from a dream
And wondered what that dream could mean.
Then 'Hurry up' shouted Mum,
'We're going on holiday to Earth.'

Jennifer Southall (10)
Yarlside School

Cosmic

I'm flying through the universe, the wonderful marvellous universe,
The things I do, the things I see
On earth I played and ran with glee.
When I looked into the sky at night,
I wondered what it would be like,
To fly through space.

Now I'm gliding throughout space,
I look at the earth and think,
I used to gaze into the sky and wonder what it would be like,
To fly through space.

I glance at all the planets,
There's too many to count,
Jupiter, Mars, Pluto, the Moon,
I'm soaring through the universe,
The wonderful marvellous universe.

Katy Walker (11)
Yarlside School

Cosmic

My friend has been to the moon,
he says he's been into space,
he says he's been over to Mars,
in his model rocket.

He says he's seen aliens,
living on the planets,
he says he crashed his rocket
on the planet Jupiter.

He says the moon is made of cheese,
he says he took a bite,
but do you think I believed him,
no, I'm not that daft.

I think he told a lie,
I think he was joking around,
but are there aliens out in space,
living on the planets?

Liam Roberts (11)
Yarlside School

STRAY SATELLITE

A satellite was whizzing round
and round the Earth,
Transmitting signals here and there,
When it suddenly struck a stray planet,
And went spinning everywhere.
It rocketed past Jupiter,
It tumbled past Saturn,
The satellite nearly collided with the moon,
And finally twisting and turning,
It crashed into the middle of Sahara Desert,
Leaving all the little people in front of their TVs,
Looking at the inquisitive wildlife of Africa.

Benjamin Shaw (10)
Yarlside School